Identity Management

A Business Perspective

Graham Williamson

MC Press Online, LLC
Boise, ID 83703 USA

Identity Management: A Business Perspective

Graham Williamson

First Edition

First Printing—February 2017

MC Press offers excellent discounts on this book when ordered in quantity for bulk purchases or special sales, which may include custom covers and content particular to your business, training goals, marketing focus, and branding interest.

MC Press Online, LLC
Corporate Offices: 3695 W. Quail Heights Court, Boise, ID 83703-3861 USA
Sales and Customer Service: (208) 629-7275 ext. 500; service@mcpressonline.com
Permissions and Bulk/Special Orders: mcbooks@mcpressonline.com
www.mcpressonline.com • www.mc-store.com

ISBN: 978-1-58347-499-0

Contents

Contents

Preface

In the years since the book I coauthored, *Identity Management: A Primer*, was published, the identity and access management task has become significantly more complex, and an order of magnitude more important. It has become more complex because of the cloud and the necessity to support mobile devices. It has become more important because the networking solutions of yesteryear are no longer sufficient.

This book seeks to assist the chief information officer (CIO), or better still the chief digital officer (CDO), in grappling with this complexity and leveraging the organization's identity data to deploy an efficient and secure information technology (IT) environment. Organizations that can accomplish this can potentially realize significant benefits: better staff relations, more secure contractor engagement, more profitable customer relationships, and empowered business units that can finally get real-time information on inventory levels, production rates, market prices, and customer satisfaction. For those organizations that fail to address the identity management challenge, the term "digital transformation" will have a special meaning.

Ten years ago, identity and access management (IAM) was nicely compartmentalized and relatively easy to understand. There were a dozen vendors in the market, and after determining a company's size and propensity for an enterprise directory, as a consultant it was relatively easy for me to define a solution. I enjoyed visiting clients, listening to how vendors had bamboozled them, and explaining a succinct way forward to reach their IAM goals.

Then the "cloud" arrived.

Suddenly, it was necessary to throw out the old paradigm of enterprise directories and firewalls at the perimeter and figure out how to avoid opening up the enterprise directory to the world. At the same time, it was necessary to determine how to support software as a service (SaaS) applications without synchronizing identity data to the cloud. With the HR and identity management (IdM) systems on the internal network and the SaaS applications on the Internet, some "magic" was needed. But solutions were available, and cloud providers started supporting identity in the cloud and the SAML protocol, to varying degrees.

Then came BYOD.

All of a sudden, users were coming from anywhere with a wide variety of devices. They could no longer be relied upon to use the company's standard operating environment (SOE). No longer were they inside the corporate network, and their devices could be used by anyone at any time of the day or night.

But solutions have developed rapidly. There are now new ways of supporting access from anywhere by anyone at any time. The development of protocols such as OpenID Connect and OAuth and initiatives such as Fast IDentity Online (FIDO) provide solid security for external access to protected corporate systems and data.

Now the Internet of Things (IoT) is upon us: how do we manage the identity of things? How do we allow secure access to corporate facilities? And what about blockchain technology? Is it appropriate for situations where components of identity can be distributed across multiple data repositories?

It is important that we keep up with technological developments and extend our frameworks to understand these challenges and take advantage of the attendant opportunities.

Identity Management from a Business Perspective

This book seeks to make sense of identity management: where it has come from and where it's going. It's written at a business person level because it is important that business people understand identity management.

It's the level at which decisions should be made as to the strategy to follow to develop our cybersecurity infrastructure and competence. We can no longer afford to have the C-suite abrogate their responsibility and expose their organizations to unnecessary risk. Now is the time to address identity management, understand its potential, and set our organizations on a trajectory to leverage the promise it affords.

This book seeks only to make identity management understandable. It will be the CIO's responsibility to decide what this means and set their organization on a well-thought-out path to robust security at an affordable cost.

In 2002, US Secretary of Defense Donald Rumsfeld uttered a truism that is often quoted but never more appropriate to the identity and access management situation in most companies today: there are "known knowns," "known unknowns," and "unknown unknowns."

The "known knowns" are the tried and true identity management tools and standard processes, such as provisioning user accounts in Microsoft Active Directory (AD). The "known unknowns" are the issues around provisioning to cloud applications and support for mobile devices. The "unknown unknowns" are ways to manage IoT devices to truly secure our corporate environment. We know we need to get ready to do this, we know we need to share corporate information with staff and business partners, but we don't know how to do it. Do we need to purchase a secure information sharing solution, and if so, would the staff use it? Do we need to expose an API for IoT devices; if so, who sets the guidelines for security and management? Do we need to provide better services for consumers; if so, how do we identify them and still adhere to privacy regulation?

In this book, we'll address these questions, while keeping technical detail to a minimum, and we will endeavor to appreciate the opportunities that a good identity and access management environment affords.

Chapter 1 looks at the changes that have happened and increasingly impact our security environment, and how we can leverage our IdM environment.

Chapter 2 looks at the provisioning task, so we can determine the features we need, in order to ensure correct access permissions are assigned to users.

Chapter 3 discusses directories. If there is any area of our identity management environment that is changing in the fast-paced development of IAM, it is directories.

Chapter 4 sorts out the issues affecting authorization and authentication. We'll take a look at current trends and determine what's most important in our environment.

Chapter 5 addresses the cloud and notes the impact it is having on IAM systems.

Chapter 6 discusses the use of mobile devices and investigates the wisdom, or otherwise, of supporting bring your own device (BYOD).

Chapter 7 focuses on IoT and how it impacts identity.

Chapter 8 addresses the importance of IAM for industrial computer systems and the roadblocks to exploiting corporate IAM facilities.

Chapter 9 is devoted to secure information sharing and how it should be part of an organization's data loss prevention strategy.

Chapter 10 is about consumerization, its impact on IAM, and how to "know your customer."

Chapter 11 discusses regulation and its impact on our IAM strategy.

Chapter 12 looks forward to the issues that will affect our IAM environments in the next few years and how we should prepare for them.

Each chapter consists of content on the topic in question, a use case analysis to help our understanding, and a question and answer section to promote discussion.

The expectation is that the reader will begin reading the book having some appreciation of the identity management topic, and will have a better appreciation of identity management after reading the book. The reader may not find all chapters to be equally useful, but my intent is that the majority of this book's content will provide business value. No doubt there will be areas of disagreement—but that's good. It is only after having our understanding challenged that our ideas become stronger and more actionable. That's my hope: to stimulate action in developing corporate strategy.

As one wise professor once told me, "If you're not going to do anything, you don't need a strategy."

Best wishes,

Graham Williamson

Chapter 1

An Update

There's little doubt that managing identities is becoming increasingly important. As the network perimeter becomes fuzzier, the ability of organizations to limit access to protected resources based on network controls is becoming more and more difficult. With much access control occurring in the cloud, now a new model is required that leverages identity data to determine user entitlements for access to protected resources. The Internet of Things (IoT) complicates access control further because now it is necessary to control access to things and manage data coming from things.

Consumerization is another significant trend that will shape society over the next few years. This trend very much depends upon a model that allows us to know our customers so that we can provide them the experience that they expect.

So: identity is important. The way we manage identities is rapidly changing, and access control has become a business imperative. The task is to understand our identity management environment and the possibilities that exist, and to take a strategic approach to planning the development of that environment.

What Is an Identity?

I don't know how many times I have heard someone say that they have multiple identities.

Unless they are a secret agent with multiple passports or a criminal with multiple bank accounts in different names, this is not so. As individuals, each of us must, by definition, have only one identity. Although we will have different attributes in different domains, an individual is one person with one identity.

For an example, let's consider someone who is a teacher. The attributes that define a teacher, beyond the biographical details of name, address, age, and gender, are items such as his or her role within the school, subjects he or she teaches, and maybe a credential for extracurricular activities in which he or she is involved. These attributes will determine the level of access the teacher gets to the school's systems. A teacher does not need wide access to school systems, only access to the grades and subjects he or she is teaching. A department head would get greater access than an intern teacher; the coach of the rowing team would get access to the team details and competition schedule. So ensuring a teacher's identity attributes in the identity management system is essential to implementing a robust and secure authentication system.

But what if the teacher was also a parent with children in the same school? Now the school needs to know details such as student name, class, and guardian status. The teacher is still a teacher; he or she is also a parent, but the parent and teacher are one identity.

It gets more complicated: the teacher is also a bank customer with a bank account. The bank obviously needs to know the person's biographical data, too, but not the classes she teaches or teams she coaches. The bank does care about banking domain attributes such as account number, account balance, overdraft history, and creditworthiness.

So, in the teaching domain the teacher has attributes, in the parent domain he or she has different attributes, and in the banking domain yet more attributes—but the individual is still one person and one identity. An identity management system must be able to manage this complexity.

Definitions

It's appropriate at this point to define some terms and agree on the terminology we are going to use. *Identity management* (IdM) is only part of the *identity and access management* (IAM) task. While managing identities is an important activity in and of itself, one of the main purposes of identity management is to control access to protected resources. We need to keep both sides of the equation balanced: a focus on only identity management ignores the reason for doing it in the first place; but if access control becomes the prime focus, we might not adequately address the need to manage identities. We need to treat them as two sides of the same coin.

Identity Management Defined

One of the best definitions of identity management I've come across is this:

> *Identity management is the administrative discipline that collects, stores, uses, and discards data that identifies persons or things in a particular jurisdiction in accordance with pertinent policy and regulatory controls.*

This means an identity management facility must have:

- An administrative capability with trained staff and a management console of some type
- A storage facility that can accommodate and protect the identity data
- A policy definition capability that provides guidance on how protected data is to be treated
- Recognition of regulation that affects the management of identity data and a mechanism to demonstrate adherence

In many cases, identity management environments fail to provide these requirements, thus hindering the organization's ability to adequately manage identity data. Some typical shortcomings are:

- A poor provisioning system that does not provide user self-service and approval workflows
- A poor de-provisioning capability that fails to disable accounts when a staff member leaves the company
- Identity data spread over multiple locations and no single management function to update identity data as it changes. Staff members are required to update data in multiple places when they change their home address or phone number.
- Lack of a cloud strategy to avoid proliferation of data stores across multiple cloud service providers
- A board of directors whose only IT policy is a "permissible use statement for Internet access." Issues such as the cloud, support for mobile devices, and privacy regulation are often put in the "too hard" basket and not addressed at board level.
- Lack of accommodation for regulatory controls such as privacy legislation and a failure to adopt conforming practices

This all adds up to a situation in which C-level managers are exposing their organizations to unnecessary risk.

> One client site had problems with phone number management. New staff were issued a number by the PABX administrator, but they then had to remember to enter the number in the Global Address List in order to be contactable via the Microsoft Outlook contact directory. There was also a separate Phones directory with a separate administrator whom they needed to notify when their phone number changed. The process was improved by assigning an "authoritative source" for each identity attribute.

Access Management Defined

Gartner defines IAM as "the security discipline that enables the right individuals to access the right resources at the right times for the right reasons." Figure 1.1 illustrates the IAM process.

Figure 1.1: Identity Access Management (IAM) process

This is a good definition because it not only presumes an identity management capability, it focuses on access management. It recognizes that there are protected resources, times at which access should occur and times when it should not, and that there must be a reason for access to be granted. So IAM includes the other side of the equation: once we've managed our identities, we need to determine what we can let them do.

On the identity management side, we need to ensure that identity information is accurately and securely collected with appropriate approval received and recorded for all access requested. On the access management side, the task is to manage the authentication of users to protected resources. This could be computer systems, computer programs, document stores, or physical access controls such as door locks. It is equally important that the identity management side can de-provision a person when they leave the organization to ensure that the access management side can no longer grant access to protected resources.

It is only when the two sides of the equation are balanced that business processes can leverage the IAM environment to drive productivity and profitability. If the provisioning is not happening securely, access control will be hindered; if access control procedures don't leverage a robust IdM infrastructure, protected resources could be compromised.

The Components of IAM

At a high level, there are only a few components of a robust identity and access management environment that need to be addressed in the IAM strategy: provisioning, authentication, and authorization.

Provisioning

The term *provisioning* in an identity management sense refers to the process of enrolling a new staff member or contractor to give them access to the systems and applications they need to perform their jobs. It is sometimes called *onboarding*.

The task is a joint human resources (HR) and IT responsibility and ideally should be integrated with the recruitment process. Increasingly contractor provisioning is required, and such provisioning might be an HR function or a finance function, depending on which area of the business is responsible for contractors. Unfortunately, the HR department often does not want to deal with contractors because they have enough to do managing staff. The job then falls to finance because they manage contractor payments. This is not ideal because the finance department is typically not equipped to manage individual contractor issues such as access to computer systems and other protected assets. Ideally contractors should be managed via the HR system because they have similar system access assignments, job training credential management, and asset management issues. But in some cases, HR system licensing is based on user numbers, and it is unwise to manage contracts this way. In this case, a contractor management system, under HR control, should be deployed.

Provisioning should be as automated as much as possible and should involve a workflow-based process to collect approvals for system access. Approvals can be a person's manager, the system that manages the applications to which access has been requested, or a delegate who is tasked with approving system access for the department or workgroup to which the person belongs. Upon a staff member's exit from a company, a workflow should disable a former employee's account to ensure his or her system access is removed.

Attestation reporting, whereby a manager is advised of their subordinate's system access, is increasingly important and must be provided by any identity management system deployed today. The provisioning engine should log all approved access requests, and attestation reports should be selectable by a manager, work group, or department. The organization should conduct a recertification process periodically to verify system access for staff.

Authentication

Authentication involves validating a person's identity so that access rights to a computer network, computer system, or another protected resource can be determined. In some cases, it is used to refer to access being granted to an application—that is, the user "authenticates" to the financial administration system, but this is getting close to authorization.

Authentication systems today are more complex than in the past because identity management environments are increasingly being called upon to authenticate access from locations external to the corporate facilities—that is, users who connect to corporate systems from home or another remote location. It is no longer possible to rely on an 802.*x* network login to a wireless LAN. Now connections are coming in via the Internet, and a method to "authenticate" users is required. This may be via a Web server that presents a login screen to authenticate a user via a public identity provider service (i.e., social login), or it may authenticate the user to their organization's directory service.

Organizations are increasingly taking a risk management approach to authentication; for example, a wireless LAN login during business hours from a corporate PC is considered lower risk than a login via the Internet from a mobile device, late at night. This means that modern protocols such as OpenID Connect and OAuth tokens are increasingly important and must be supported in order to secure access from remote devices (see chapter 4 for more detail).

Users who access cloud apps also need to authenticate. Thus, identity provider services must support protocols such as SAML to allow an HTTP session to authenticate.

Federated Authentication

Increasingly businesses need to give access to business partners or contractor staff. In the past, a system administrator typically added business partners to the organization's internal directory to allow them access to appropriate services. This is not only time consuming, but it also leads to orphaned accounts and increased risk with external account access not properly managed. Federation is the preferred solution whereby the corporate IdM environment "trusts" the external party's identity service and logs their users into the corporate network or application on the basis of their home organization's IdP.

Authorization

Authorization is the granting or denial of access to computer applications or other protected resources in accordance with policy. Access can be granted on a more fine-grained basis by evaluating more identity and context attributes when making an access control decision. For instance, if a doctor requests access to a specialized health management application, the authorization system should check the doctor's medical credentials and his/her training accreditation on the specialized hardware.

Authorization systems are typically characterized by externalization of decision making and centralization of policy management. This means that the organization's applications must remove access control logic and add enforcement point code that can communicate with a decision-point service for a permit or deny decision. It also requires policies to be established in the decision point to be able to determine the requesting user's entitlement to access the protected resource (see chapter 4 for more detail).

Provisioning System Capabilities

There is a wide disparity in the levels of sophistication and capability between provisioning systems within organizations. Figure 1.2 shows these different levels.

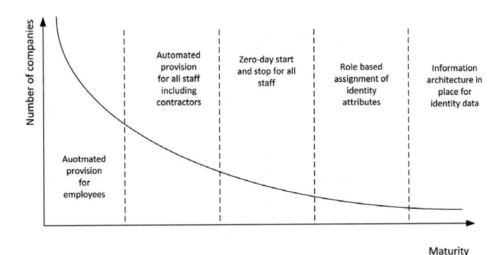

Figure 1.2: Provisioning system sophistication

There are multiple reasons that organizations fail to develop modern and sophisticated provisioning systems that leverage their identity data repositories to improve business practices:

- Lack of motivation to correct poor business practices. This issue can often be traced to the HR department, which typically considers its primary responsibility to be managing payroll rather than managing identities within the company.
- Fragmented management, where no one in the company is responsible for identity management and for the protection of personally identifiable information (PII).
- Lack of policy direction in the organization, with no high-level responsibility for IdM issues.
- Lack of understanding in the company in regard to the capabilities of current IdM technology and its importance in the modern organization.

In many cases, business managers are unaware of the changes in technology that now make IdM a viable option for small organizations. Whereas a few years ago, it was typically difficult to justify the deployment of an IdM system in a company with fewer than 10,000 employees, organizations with as few as 1,000 employees can now afford a full-featured IdM system.

Although there are many large organizations that use provisioning solutions, far fewer are making good use of a full-featured IdM solution to save costs and improve business processes.

Level 1: Staff Provisioning

Most large companies have at least a basic system to automatically write entries to an identity store within the organization when new staff are entered into the HR system. There is a mechanism to take an HR record and move pertinent data to a directory or database that constitutes a repository of staff contact details in the company. Most of organizations provision into Active Directory (AD), or another network directory, directly and also into the company's email server. In some cases, an application such as Outlook becomes the contact tool for the organization, although this can limit the staff detail that can be provided because AD is an authentication directory, and typically lacks the amount of data required for a contact directory (see chapter 3 for more detail).

Beyond this, many companies provision into other applications manually, rather than deploy a workflow engine to provision into computer systems automatically. This typically represents a significant cost for an organization and elevates its risk profile, since de-provisioning is difficult.

Level 2: Contractor Provisioning

Many companies still have no automated provisioning system for contractors. This is a serious impediment to proper identity management. The source of the problem is typically the HR departments that still see themselves as managing payroll. Since contractors are typically paid through the finance system, most HR departments disavow any knowledge of them.

More enlightened HR departments see themselves as the owner of identity management for the organization and willingly take on the role of managing the commencement and cessation of duties for contractor staff as well as employees.

> Identity management solutions that maintain their own identity stores usually provide an interface to manage contract staff, either manually or via a contractor management system. Some vendors that have a user-based licensing model will allow contractors, who only access systems periodically, to be factored when calculating the full-time equivalent (FTE) count that determines license costs.
>
> For instance, alumni who rarely access a university system should not incur the same license cost as enrolled students.

Level 3: Zero-day Start

Being able to access corporate systems from the first day on the job is a reasonable expectation of any identity management environment. It is untenable that a member of staff should join an organization and not be able to log on because their identity record in the authorization directory has not been created. It is incumbent on a properly designed identity management environment that access should be granted on the first day of employment.

It is even more important that accounts are disabled upon cessation of duties. In today's environment, where so much external access to company resources is permitted, disabling an account on the date of exit is extremely important. Account deletions will then await the periodic "cleanup" to be fully removed from the system.

Level 4: Role-based

A role-based assignment of identity attributes is an effective way to provision new identities, and can significantly facilitate the task of managing identity provisioning. It requires a concerted effort on the part of the organization, primarily the HR department, to manage the number of unique roles within the organization. Role-based access control requires a discrete and manageable number of roles to be defined and a governance group to manage the assignment of access based on these roles.

> When a department of education in one Australian state implemented role-based access control, it found that there were over 1,500 roles for staff in schools. The decision was to dramatically reduce the number of roles. Principals were required to assign their staff to one of eight roles. For instance, only one head-of-department (HoD) role was established.
>
> Note: HoD for mathematics is the same role as HoD for physics. The department attribute determines a staff member's access rights to school file stores; thus, access should be based on the staff member's "role" and their "department" attribute.

Level 5: Architecture-based

An organization at this level indicates a high level of maturity, with identity data defined within the organization's enterprise identity architecture. This requires the complete definition of the various types of staff member and the attributes that pertain to them. An entity relationship diagram should be generated for each identity type (including organization entities, too). The entity definitions should support the business system architecture. For instance, if the security access system requires knowledge of the location in which a staff member works, to enable correct encoding of the employee's door access card, the relationship diagram must show this requirement, and the identity management environment must expose the location attribute.

So, What's New?

The demands placed on provisioning are becoming much more sophisticated and have extensive HR system integration and workflow requirements. Most organizations now have rudimentary provisioning from their HR system. Some have extended this to staff who are not in the HR system (e.g., contractors). Increasingly organizations are relying on contractor staff, so being able to manage contractors is mandatory. If this cannot be done through the HR system, deploying a contractor management system is recommended. A few organizations have taken the next step to provide authorization based on a staff member's job profile (role-based access control). Organizations are requiring sophisticated approval capabilities to accommodate configurable escalation periods, selection from a group of approvers, and parallel workflow capabilities. Logging approvals for attestation reporting is also mandatory.

Another interesting development is extending provisioning into the area of dynamic access control—that is, provisioning a person on demand. Network providers now support real-time access control where bridges and switches segment traffic not only on the basis of IP address, but also on identity attributes. For instance, a person in the finance department will get access to the Finance subnet as long as the IdM system indicates they are finance department staff. This can be especially useful in the area of system support. Restricted areas such as log-file systems can be segmented based on a user's job profile, so that only system administrators gain access to protected file systems.

Authentication is increasingly being augmented with an authorization task. Separate "network logons" and application login are being replaced by a single sign-on (SSO) activity that grants users access to the resources to which they are entitled, without any subsequent authentication activity. A major driver for SSO is federation, which combines local applications with cloud-based applications in a single, secure authentication and authorization environment.

Much is now happening in the area of entitlement management based on identity attributes. There is an accelerating move away from developing software programs with embedded access control features to externalizing access decisions to authorization servers that leverage the company's identity management system. New applications simply expose a standards-based access control enforcement point that looks to a decision point in the identity provider service. On request, the decision point responds to the application with a "permit," "deny," or "indeterminate" access control decision. The main benefit of the new entitlement methodology is the centralization of policies. A single set of access policies can now control access decisions across the entire application portfolio (see chapter 4 for more detail).

Governance is another area that is developing rapidly. To date, most organizations have neglected to provide their managers with the access management information necessary to do their jobs. This is now changing, and the need for attestation reporting has been recognized as essential. Vendors are building better reporting capabilities into their identity management products, including built-in recertification functionality. This means that managers will get periodic attestation reports that require them to check the access their staff has to various applications and "attest" to its accuracy. Validated access will be recertified with a timestamp that indicates the date and time the access was reapproved. Rescinded access will be acted on automatically: the user's ID will be removed from the relying application or AD group.

Another component of governance is analytics and dashboards. Increasingly CIOs and IT managers now want a real-time display of provisioning rates, authentication loads, and login failures, with the ability to drill down to determine causal agents.

Major Trends

Identity Is the New Security

In the past, network security could be relied upon to provide the security we needed; we would protect the network via our local network directory, which would authenticate a user and allow them access to the network. But that's no longer sufficient, since many connections to our protected resources are not from within the corporate network and might be from devices outside our direct control, such as a smartphone. Now we need to manage a person's access based on their identity and related credentials; there are no longer boundaries around our corporate information network, and we must allow access from remote locations using mobile devices. Our users also want to access software applications in the cloud, so we must accommodate cloud applications by providing access to our identity directory, but this must be done securely. An LDAP interface should not be exposed over the Internet (see chapter 3).

> An Australian university recently installed a federated authentication tool that controls access to the university's portal and computer programs, whether they are on the local network or in a cloud infrastructure. The federation provides a single security domain with no requirements for university identities to be sent to external applications or identity stores. Single sign-on to applications is enjoyed by staff and students, regardless of the location of the program.

Cloud

One of the more profound impacts that technology development is having on identity management is the migration of information technology services to the cloud. As organizations embrace cloud-based infrastructure and applications, it is important that the identity management environment is planned accordingly. On-premises identity provider services are not appropriate to support cloud-based applications, and synchronizing identity data to cloud apps raises security issues. Typically, organizations should establish an identity service, under their control, and require all cloud-based systems to authenticate with the service; that is, identity data should not be stored by cloud apps (see chapter 5).

Another consideration is the potential use of public identity-provider services such as GoogleID, Facebook, LinkedIn, or Microsoft Live. If the population that needs to be authenticated is large, and the assurance level of the application being accessed is low, the use of such "social logins" is an obvious choice. It allows identification of the user without having to establish an identity data store. If, on the other hand, a higher level of authentication is required—for instance, to access sensitive information or to submit an application, a social login will not be satisfactory because the registration process that a public IdP undertakes is generally not sufficient. In this case, the authentication must be augmented by an additional process that verifies the user's identity to a greater degree.

It is important, then, for any cloud migration strategy development to include identity management as part of the plan.

Internet of Things (IoT)

With the arrival of IoT, we must get better at managing entities as well as identities. We need to know who owns these "things," who should get access to the data they collect, and who should be able to control them. To try and achieve this without a robust IAM environment is an endeavor fraught with difficulty and unnecessarily exposes an organization to risk.

There are two aspects of IoT that impact identity management. First is the access that IoT devices might need to corporate systems. If a device collects data—for example, measuring temperature or counting boxes, the data will be written to a repository of some kind. This means that the corporate data security model must be revised to include these "entities" with access control policy, and potentially encryption services that mirror the identity management model. In other words, if a user must digitally sign their access requests to a database, so should a device. While key management for "things" will likely differ, signing and encryption should not.

The other issue is providing access to devices that are being used to monitor something or control something. In the former case, the device "owner" should be able to determine where data is stored and with whom it is shared. In the latter case, only approved personnel should gain access to the control device, for obvious reasons. In both cases, the corporate identity service is a critical component.

Consumerization

Along with driverless cars and in-home medical devices, consumerization will undoubtedly have a major effect on our lives over the next few years. As organizations respond to changing demographics—from baby boomers who want low prices and good deals, to millennials who want a good experience, the face of customer service will improve. To accomplish this, organizations will increasingly rely on their identity management environment to support better customer interactions with advanced "know your customer" environments.

As we access services from banks, shops, governments, and health care organizations, we will increasingly require more personalized service and organizations that will need to better manage what they know about us, and tailor their services accordingly. This raises a major concern for organizations in dealing with the public; ensuring adherence to privacy legislation is a necessity.

Software-Defined Networking (SDN)

Computer network technology continues to advance at an accelerating pace. Software-defined networking (SDN) and its cousin network function virtualization (NFV) have completely redefined networking over the past few years. Many network equipment suppliers such as Cisco, EMC, and Dell have delivered agile network devices that are fully configurable to undertake a wide variety of network tasks. It's now possible to define network segments and control access to them entirely in software that leverages the organization's network directory.

This makes an organization's identity provider service front and center of the security task. If the IdP is not accurate and current, the organization's security will be compromised and the risk profile will rise.

Role of the CIO

The CIO's role within organizations is becoming more critical as the need for better identity management increases. It is the CIO who must provide the provisioning infrastructure and drive the organization to clean up the number of roles it maintains, to enable the necessary attributes to be set within the identity stores, so that authentication and authorization tasks can be adequately completed. This is an information architecture task that is part of the enterprise architecture for which the CIO is responsible. With the changes required in the authorization area, it is again the CIO's responsibility to set the direction for the company and explain to the board of directors the importance of a coherent IdM facility.

Finally, it is the CIO who must determine the governance required in the identity management space. The responsibility to ensure that the IdM environment provides the necessary information to allow the identity management task to be properly managed falls to the CIO. And it's the CIO who will enable upper management to understand who is on staff, what access they have, and who approved the access, and ensure that system access is removed if and when appropriate.

Consumer Concerns

The requirements of consumers are sometimes lost in the focus on corporate requirements and business opportunities. Recognizing consumer needs and wants when developing business strategy is now an essential component of any IT strategy development. On the one hand, this attention to consumer needs enables an organization to avoid infringing an individual's rights and the potential consequences of such infringement. On the other hand, it means that the organization can leverage and exploit "know your customer" facilities to drive business enablement.

Users cannot be expected to understand the intricacies of systems and their capability to manage their own identity settings. Consumers expect that the organizations with which they do business will protect their sensitive data and their privacy rights. Complex terms and conditions in end-user licensing agreements are attracting the ire of users today, so that organizations that rely on pages of fine print to protect their interests are vulnerable to litigation. Lawyers are increasingly relying on the "reasonable person" argument to negate protection that relies on users' understanding of an unduly complex agreement.

The focus these days needs to be user experience. Those companies that can provide a good user experience are destined for greater prosperity as satisfied customers go on social media to relate their experience; those companies that fail to leverage their customer data to provide a good user experience are likely to fall victim to "digital transformation." A disappointed customer no longer writes a letter; they tweet or blog to the world about disappointment.

Conclusion

There's a lot happening in the IdM sector. Identity management is changing rapidly, and its importance is increasing as cloud applications and network device technology develop and evolve. CIOs can no longer afford to ignore the IdM task and take an out-of-sight, out-of-mind approach. Identity management has been raised to a mission-critical status, not only for business protection, but for business enablement as well.

Never has there been a more exciting time to be involved in identity management. As security solutions increasingly look to identity repositories for access control purposes, it's important to ensure that our identity data is accurately and efficiently collected and managed to heighten security within our organization and to drive down costs.

Q & A

Q. Has the CIO's job morphed into a chief digital officer (CDO) role?

A. Yes. There are two drivers for the migration of the CIO role:

The board of directors needs to be informed about, and make decisions in regard to, defining policy for access control within the organization. To leave this policy definition task up to the IT department is an abrogation of responsibility. This means that the CIO needs to extend his or her focus beyond access control to business facilitation (e.g., managing supplier access to inventory levels).

If the CIO remains IT focused, the organization will miss out on an important competitive advantage opportunity. Technology can assist business units in developing capability that will drive new business opportunities and directly impact the bottom line—for example, by providing access to real-time production rates. The corollary is: if the CIO fails to assist the organization to "digitally transform," soon there may be no organization left to manage.

This means that CIOs have to progress from just managing IT to helping business units to leverage all aspects of digital technology to drive business enablement. Therefore, the CIO role is really a CDO who stays abreast of technology developments and helps business units to understand their potential and to deploy them, if required.

Q. Can an effective access control system be deployed in the absence of a robust IdM infrastructure?

A. No. Access control is a business function; that is, the business units should determine who can access their applications. Without an up-to-date and accurate IdM environment, business units will establish their own access control system— that is, they will expend resources to maintain lists that will grant entitlements.

There are two problems with this: 1) it is impossible to provide a corporate-wide view of access control, and 2) business units must remember to remove a person's access when it is no longer required.

If individual business units are determining access control policy in isolation from the rest of the company, inconsistencies will arise and the cost of governance will be unnecessarily elevated.

It is therefore imperative that a current, well-developed identity management environment is in place to support access control within an organization.

Q. What facilities should business application owners demand from their IdM environments?

A. Ideally the provisioning of new staff and contractors should be a corporate function with a single provisioning environment to provide a company-wide facility for enrolling new staff. But this should include an approval workflow that involves the business units. This workflow must require the business units to be actively engaged in setting the permissions of staff who require access to their applications and in ensuring the veracity of the approval workflows—who can approve the granting of access rights to each application.

This also means that the business units should be included in establishing corporate governance over access control processes; they become engaged in ensuring that security process and procedures are followed and in establishing corporate-wide access control policy.

Business application owners should be involved in the deployment of the IdM environment, so that they understand its capabilities and to ensure their requirements are considered in any development activity.

Chapter 2

Identity and Access Management

There are many configurations of identity and access management (IAM) systems, and to some extent, each organization's IAM system will be unique, developed and deployed to suit the organization's own specific requirements. But all systems do need a provisioning tool, a data store, and one or more access control facilities.

IAM Core Capabilities

There are six core features of an identity and access management (IAM) environment; this chapter will look at how they have developed over the past few years and what should be expected of any new deployments. Figure 2.1 illustrates a simplified IAM environment, showing these core features.

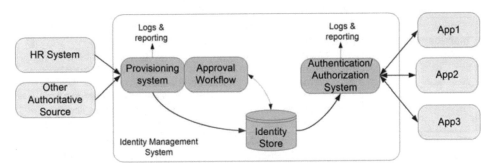

Figure 2.1: Simplified IAM environment

Table 2.1 summarizes the capabilities of the six core features. (We'll explore these in more detail later in this chapter.)

Table 2.1: Core features of an IAM environment

Core Feature	Description
Provisioning and human resource management system (HRMS) integration	The input to an identity store is via some form of provisioning tool. This can be an application form that is placed on a help desk queue or sent to a system administrator to be actioned. Preferably, this will be an online form, which can 1) ensure that all the relevant data has been collected and 2) apply some "rules" to determine the data repositories to write user data to. In some cases, this will be to an access control list (ACL) within an application. In other cases, it will be an Active Directory (AD) group, and in other cases it will remain in the identity store for access by an authentication system.
Approval workflow and self-service	Identity management (IdM) systems incorporate a workflow system to collect approvals for the requested system access entitlements. This approval might be granted by a user's manager, a system owner, or a departmental delegate, depending on the access control policy set by the organization. Applications should be entered by the requesting staff member, not their manager or clerical staff, in order to eliminate keying errors and the cost of administration.
Role optimization and entitlement management	The workflow should, ideally, have role optimization built into the rules, which simplifies the granting of entitlements and enables business units to coordinate the combination of access rights to eliminate high-risk entitlements (i.e., those that might break separation-of-duties constraints).
Access management	There is a range of access management models that might need to be supported. The two most common models are AD groups, whereby a user's ID is written to the AD group membership for the system(s) they are entitled to access, or a Web access management facility that manages access to multiple Web-based applications. Increasingly, applications are relying on authentication/authorization systems that access the identity store to determine a user's attributes during the login procedure.
Attestation reporting and governance, risk management, and compliance (GRC)	At the very least, IAM systems must provide attestation reports that are sent periodically to managers with a request for them to check the access rights of their staff and attest to the fact that it is correct. Today's IAM systems will often include recertification facilities to update entries that are wrong or need changing. Reporting functions also support audits and other governance activities.
Analytics and dashboard	Modern IAM systems include out-of-the box analytics and dashboard functionality that management can use to monitor the efficacy of the IAM system and to identify conditions that are causing delays or indicate surreptitious activity.

Significant progress has been made in each of these areas, some more than others, and we need to ensure we leverage this new capability.

Provisioning

The provisioning activity is a core function of an identity management system. It is the act of establishing records in the organization's identity store(s), adding a new user to the identity store facility to give them access to an application, a system, or a protected resource. It could be as simple as adding a user's unique identifier to an AD group or as complex as making an entry in an application's database to grant a new user the required level of access.

Many organizations use Microsoft's AD, NetIQ eDirectory, Oracle Unified Directory, or another directory or database product to store staff data. *Provisioning* is the act of entering this data for new employees and establishing their entitlements. *De-provisioning* is the act of removing data for staff who leave the company, which will remove their access permissions. It is important that provisioning occur as soon as possible, so that the new employee can log in to systems on his or her first day of work (sometimes called *zero-day start*). It is even more important that a staff member's access is disabled as soon as they leave an organization's employ.

> The source of provisioning data is typically the company's human resources (HR) system. Generally, this is the "authoritative source" of most identity data.

Authoritative data sources are typically the systems used to initially collect data; they are production systems that should not be used by other applications for identity management purposes. This is the function of the "source of truth" for the enterprise, which is typically a directory that serves as the identity repository for systems and applications in the enterprise.

A provisioning tool will add, change, or remove identity attributes, with the appropriate approval, in the authoritative data sources. If data is changed in an authoritative source, it is detected and copied to dependent identity stores via a synchronization tool that moves the new data out to the appropriate identity stores. The provisioning tool is interfaced to all the identity stores it provisions into and provides reporting and reconciliation functions to ensure that data integrity is maintained.

In the past, this synchronization would be performed nightly, whereby the identity management tool would interrogate the HR system and write updates to the identity repository. Increasingly this is becoming a real-time operation, where updates occur on event (i.e., when the HR system records a change).

Most organizations have a provisioning tool that automatically onboards new employees, based on their employment record in the HR system. The HR system is the logical source of identity data since it is the place where employee information (e.g., name, address, date of birth) is collected and assigned to a department and position.

The next step is to use this identity information to provision staff accounts in the computer systems that they need to access. In many instances, an employee's position can be used to determine the access they should be granted to applications and systems that are used in performing the role to which they have been assigned. Typically, there is also a mechanism in place to automatically create a home drive for a new employee, and an email address, too, but the provisioning system needs to go further than that. Once a person's job is defined, they should automatically get access to the systems they need for their job responsibilities. This task should not be left up to a manual process, for several reasons:

- It wastes too much time on the part of the system administrator and staff, who do not want to spend time filling in forms to get access to the required systems.

- As soon as someone has to key in information, errors can be introduced; the best person to enter the name correctly is the employee.

- If account details are entered manually, someone must remember to remove the person's access when they leave the company.

Provisioning data should also be collected as early in the onboarding process as possible. If an organization uses a recruiting system into which applicants enter their biographic detail, this record should be used to establish the HR system record, which should then become the authoritative record for the provisioning system.

At a recent assignment at a large airline in Asia, an audit picked up a severe failure in the identity management environment. It was found that there were three times as many accounts in the organization's AD than there were staff members. An investigation revealed that a system modification that had been performed on the 10-year-old, homegrown identity management system had broken the de-provisioning feature, and accounts were no longer removed when staff left the airline's employ. The system had no documentation, and the application was no longer manageable.

Approval Workflow and Self-service

Some managers are fearful when they hear about automating their company's provisioning process. It conjures up visions that anyone will be able to request and gain access to a protected resource. Nothing could be further from the truth; automated provisioning means that the collection of user data, approval of access, and addition of the user's ID in the repository of approved users all happen automatically. All access requests must receive appropriate approval before being acted upon.

Today's identity management systems must support a workflow capability that accommodates the activities shown in Table 2.2.

Table 2.2: Identity management workflow

Activity	Description
User entry of details	The user is the best person to enter his or her details into an identity management system. The user generally knows how to spell his or her name and address correctly, which will avoid rekeying errors. The user can also be required to provide all the necessary information to substantiate his or her account establishment, avoiding a costly administration effort to chase information that should have been provided with the initial request.

Activity	Description
	Table 2.2 continued
Approval workflow	Ensuring that all user requests are appropriately approved is an important component of any provisioning system. A workflow must be configured to properly apply the approval rules established by the business. The requirement could be a manager's approval for the requested access, system manager approval, or in sensitive situations, two approvals might be required. In some cases, approvals can be granted from a "pool" of managers—for example, approval by two of five managers might be required. Knowing whom to escalate approvals to is also important. These rules need to be configured into the workflow engine. The result is that all system access will be properly approved and logged, with access entitlements granted according to corporate policy.
Entitlement catalog	As a user selects his or her required system access, the workflow needs to know the options for the requested service. The workflow can then display the options to be selected by the requestor. This means that the workflow engine must know the entitlements available within the various applications to which a user can request access. The workflow should be able to provision these entitlements either via an AD group or directly into the target application's user account repository. Ideally the IdM directory or authorization service should be used (see chapter 4 for more detail).

> In one state government health department that used a manual provisioning process, a survey of clerical staff identified that it took, on average, four queries of the data provided in a health professional's application for system access, before the application could be acted upon. In the worst case, it took 12 queries to correct errors and collect sufficient data for the provisioning activity.

A good workflow solution presupposes a relatively sophisticated identity management environment:

1. The workflow configuration must be able to identify the approval requirements for the requested access. For instance, if a new user starts as an accounts payable clerk in the finance department, the workflow must be configured to route the approval request to the finance manager. In some cases, there will be multiple approvers. In most cases, the approval request will need to be escalated to the manager's supervisor if it is not approved within a certain timeframe. There are multiple ways in

which this may be achieved: via a reference table of authorized approvers, via the "manager-is" setting in a user's directory entry, or to a defined delegate authorized to approve system access for a department or workgroup.

2. Access to a user repository of user attributes, typically a directory, is required by the authorization service. This data will normally be collected via the provisioning system and written to a directory. This data can then be leveraged by relying-on applications when a login request is received. For instance, if an application login requires a second factor such as a PIN sent to the user's mobile phone, the provisioning system should capture the mobile device number at the point of provisioning and write it to the directory as a user attribute.

3. Access to a set of challenge-response questions to validate a user's identity might be required by the workflow engine. Challenge-response questions are a common method employed to securely reset a user's password, significantly reducing password management calls to the service desk. Collecting challenge-response questions at the point of provisioning is one way to achieve this.

Role Management

A typical shortcoming in IAM environments is in the area of role management. Roles can be associated with a person's position in the company and stored as an attribute in the identity store. This can then be used for provisioning into relying applications for access control decisions. For instance, a user might need to be in the appropriate project team before they are allowed access to the team's document store; a role attribute in the identity store can be used for this purpose.

Difficulty with Roles

Role-based access control (RBAC) is often held up as the optimal approach to user provisioning. Indeed, being able to set a person's system access entitlements based on their role in the organization is a laudable objective, but there are multiple ways to do this, and they are not all equal in their efficacy or effectiveness.

Ideally roles should be attributes held against a staff member's record in the corporate directory. This attribute should instruct the provisioning workflow regarding the entitlements associated with a user's role. For instance, if a person is starting employment as a finance manager, they should get access to the finance management system with manager privileges and should be provisioned into the general ledger, accounts payable, and accounts receivable subsystems. They should also be added to the finance department's file share and the manager's corporate document repository.

Unfortunately, in many cases relying applications do not have the ability for an external workflow to set entitlements. (A *relying application* is one that relies on the corporate identity data store for access control decisions.) A common approach is to use AD groups to manage application access instead. In this instance, when a user attempts to access a specific application, or feature within an application, the system checks the AD group in question. If a user's ID is in the appropriate AD group, they will be granted the requested access; otherwise access will be denied. AD groups can be established for each application, or for each access level within a particular application, and users are provisioned into them either via a workflow or by a manual entry of the user's ID into the group. The former is preferable, but in some cases the workflow will send an email to the system owner and, if approved, the person will be manually added to the group.

The use of AD groups, even manually provisioned, is generally a better option than maintaining an access control list (ACL) within an application, access control based on roles is even better, as shown in Figure 2.2.

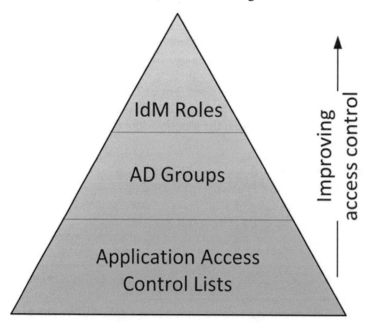

Figure 2.2: Access control hierarchy

If the groups are in AD, when the user leaves the organization their account can be disabled, which will remove their access to systems and applications. If direct entry into the application's database is used, a mechanism is required to ensure that access is removed once the staff member leaves the organization. Experience suggests that this often does not occur.

Access Management: Authentication and Authorization

The core activity of any identity management environment is to support the organization's authentication services. This most commonly refers to the logon procedure that users must complete before being granted access to a company's computing resources. User authentication is the act of verifying a person's credentials. The credentials being validated could be identity information, qualifications, or authorization level. Authentication, as the word implies, is the act of verifying a person's access entitlements as they attempt to access restricted resources.

Authorization is generally more fine-grained; it is the act of granting access to a specific resource such as a computer application or a restricted-access building. By definition, the identity management systems must be able to provide the necessary information about a person to allow the resource (e.g., computer application) to determine the correct level of access to be granted to the user. This is an area of intense change, where applications no longer maintain ACLs of users but instead rely on the identity management authorization system to make the decision regarding a user's access request (see chapter 4 for more detail).

Attestation Reporting and GRC

Anecdotal evidence suggests that fewer than 5 percent of managers receive regular reports on their staff's access entitlement to protected systems and resources. Most companies realize that this is a deficiency that requires correction. Modern IdM systems can generate attestation reports and, in many cases, implement automatic recertification whereby a user's access is confirmed and the approval is logged, and inappropriate access rights are removed.

> It is usually poor practice to rely on audit processes to identify incorrect entitlements settings. Relying on corrective action resulting from audit failures is a poor use of the audit process and will result in sub-optimal IdM management.

A common problem identified by the attestation report is "orphaned accounts," which occurs when there is a failure to remove access to a system, when a staff member leaves the company. In organizations with a good de-provisioning process, orphaned accounts are generally not a problem.

Note: Access entitlement verification should not be left to periodic audits. This is a "line" function (i.e., the responsibility of the business unit), not a "staff" function (i.e., the responsibility of a governance work group).

Governance, risk, and compliance are processes to ensure companies are not unnecessarily exposing themselves to liabilities. GRC processes are "staff" functions, not "line" functions. Ensuring that adequate governance and risk management are applied to a business process will typically fall to an administrative workgroup that will verify compliance of a line-of-business process with corporate policy. This will typically occur in a periodic audit that will report to management on any business system that is poorly designed or contravenes policy. Paradoxically, common problems are instances in which policy has not been set. Often, in the absence of policy, IT staff effectively set access control rules, and, in many companies, governance policy is not formalized, so there is no methodology to evaluate risk.

With the increasing importance of leveraging identity information, GRC requires improvement.

Analytics and Dashboard

The days of batch processes in identity management are behind us; thus, provisioning end user accounts should be a real-time process. This means that we should be able to monitor processes and report on their health continually. Most modern IdM solutions can display the number of new accounts provisioned within a configurable timeframe and alerts on events, such as denied approvals or the granting of high-risk entitlements. In addition, it is possible with most authentication services to log system access and display in real time the number of authentications to selected services.

> At an Australian university, the dashboard feature of the new IdM system allows management to view statistics on the authentication process during enrollment time, when the system access load increased by an order of magnitude. This enables the deployment of sufficient system resources to ensure satisfactory performance for all users.

Migrating to the Cloud

The accelerating use of cloud services is rapidly changing the face of identity management and complicating the provisioning task. Cloud services are often engaged by business groups without the rigorous procurement processes applied to other IT infrastructure or services. This means that integration into the company's processes and procedures is often overlooked. A common practice is to engage a cloud-based application provider and then synchronize user identities and associated attributes to the cloud. Doing so is unwise because as more services are engaged, more instances of a company's identity data store are synchronized to cloud services. The resultant proliferation of identity stores in the cloud represents a security risk and possibly a violation of privacy regulation.

Cloud IdM Service

One of the seminal activities in preparation for migrating to the cloud is to deploy a properly planned IdM service for cloud-based applications. It is not appropriate to expose the corporate directory to the Internet, for several reasons. Similarly, it is not realistic to expect a cloud-based application to send a user lookup request to the corporate network, and wait while the request transits the firewall and the load balancer before it gets serviced. Applications expect millisecond responses, which requires a planned configuration that reduces network latency to the degree possible. Since most identity stores are on-premises, this means establishing a cloud-based identity service. Many cloud service providers offer identity as a service (IDaaS) functionality. When preparing for a cloud migration, the organization will need to select an appropriate supplier to host the identity provider service and then require all software as a service (SaaS) providers to use the service. This will typically mean that all cloud-based application suppliers should support standards such as SAML for exchanging authentication messages. When selecting an identity provider supplier, it is also a good idea to stipulate support for standards such as SCIM for the exchange of identity detail.

An interesting phenomenon that we're seeing increasingly adopted within managed services environments is the trend toward industry-based federations. In such federations, multiple companies, each with its own identity provider services, operate in an industry collaboration to provide access control to information that is of importance to all the members. This is most appropriate for a cloud environment that supports an industry or supply chain in which each participant maintains its own identity provider service and each participant agrees to trust each other's identity repository. The commercial airline industry is a case in point. All major airlines participate in a system that provides access to maintenance data and other operational requirements.

One area of concern when moving to the cloud is single sign-on (SSO). SSO should be addressed; organizations with SSO for on-premises applications should not ignore this requirement when adopting cloud services. Users who have enjoyed SSO on-premises via their Web access management solution will resent the loss of this facility when moving to cloud-based services and will consider it a step backward. The cloud migration planning and selection stage should include the requirement for federation of the identity provider service (IdP) and SSO support across both on-premises and cloud services. For more detail, please refer to chapter 5.

Internet of Things

Increasingly it is necessary to support more than identities within our IAM environments. People want access to monitoring devices that collect data and to control devices that switch something on and off. The sharp reduction in the cost of such devices means that they will continue to become more accessible and economically justifiable.

This means the organization must control access to these devices and make it easy for users to share collected data securely and to delegate access to control devices when necessary. An organization's IAM environment should be the source of access control data for managing these devices.

It's equally important to protect the access from devices to corporate systems. Doing so will often require a signed/encrypted interface, which should use the same technology as interactive access (i.e., use encryption or signing keys). Consider adding devices as entities in the identity data store in order to manage certificates for encryption and digital signing. For more detail, see chapter 7.

Cloud Protocols

The development of protocols to support cloud technology and mobile devices has happened very quickly. We now have the following open standards that support these technologies.

OpenID Connect

OpenID Connect is a widely used technology for user authentication in cloud environments. It started life as OpenID, and in 2014 underwent a major release to provide more extensive functionality, which has made it the technology of choice for third-party authentication to Web applications. This makes it particularly useful for large user populations that require the use of an authentication service.

OpenID Connect is the protocol of choice to leverage public identity provider services, such as Facebook, GoogleID, and LinkedIn to authenticate users to applications. OpenID Connect lets users leverage their social network login instead of having to set up an account on a website in order to access content. This has obvious benefits when users are working from small screens that make it difficult to keep entering usernames and passwords. It also, arguably, improves security because users will not need to "write down" their login credentials.

It would be misleading to relegate OpenID Connect to the social networking space, where the level of assurance of user identities is quite low. OpenID Connect can be used in many environments where the level of assurance is defined by the robustness of the registration process used by the identity provider service. The level of assurance required by the service being accessed must be matched to the registration process of the IdP being used.

If OpenID Connect is integrated with a high-assurance service, the technology can meet enterprise-level requirements. OpenID Connect can be used with OAuth tokens issued by corporate servers to authenticate staff at high levels.

OpenID Connect is the protocol of choice to manage access from mobile devices.

OAuth

A related technology is the OAuth protocol, used for authorizing users to allow them to access a protected resource or to authenticate a device to a back-end server. OAuth's adoption has been primarily in the mobile device space, where developers want a lightweight method of access control that is appropriate for mobile phones and social login environments.

There are multiple configuration models that use either a two-legged authentication, whereby the user/device token validates the access from a mobile app, or a three-legged approach in which the "resource owner" authorizes the client to access the protected resource through a series of redirects between the target application, the user's browser or application, and the authorization server.

OAuth is often used with OpenID Connect as the authorization component of the authentication process. It is the authorization mechanism of choice for mobile devices because it is more lightweight in comparison to SAML.

FIDO

An even higher level of assurance can be provided via Fast IDentity Online (FIDO) alliance technology. While initially positioned as a password replacement technology, FIDO can go far beyond that. There are multiple solutions offered by members of the alliance, but they all adhere to the FIDO specification. Some solutions are hardware-based and require, for instance, a USB device to be plugged into the user's system to log in to a protected resource. There are also software solutions in which FIDO-compliant code is embedded in applications. The hardware device products can allow innovative solutions such as user-present functionality, requiring a user to physically touch a device in order to log in.

FIDO has been adopted by some handset manufacturers and is built into their software stack. PayPal and Google are two of the major proponents of FIDO.

Device Registration

It must be mentioned that there are other options to elevate the assurance level of access from a mobile device. Device registration immediately raises a user's level of authentication because it adds a validated second factor.

Microsoft offers a device registration service whereby only devices that have been approved can access protected resources. This can cover both on-premises and cloud applications. For cloud applications, there are additional authentication events that can be employed during the authentication process. Microsoft Azure, Amazon Web Services, and Google's cloud services all support two-factor authentication. When invoked, the authentication process will send a message to, or ring, the phone of the user and provide a PIN code that must be entered into the user's device to complete the login process. Some authentication mechanisms use a swipe or gesture to positively identify a user. The use of multiple factors during the login process significantly heightens the assurance level of the authentication[1].

Where We're Going

There is no doubt that smartphone technology is here to stay. It is also no secret that, by a long margin, more development is happening in the smartphone space than any other device type. This means that we need to develop strategies to adopt mobile devices as part of our IT environment.

---

[1] Adopting a second factor is a better mechanism for increasing the level of authentication than strengthening a single-factor mechanism—for example, forcing long passwords.

It is unlikely that smartphones will stay in their current format. As technology evolves (for example, flexible screens, wearable devices), the bits we get to interface with—screens and microphones—will evolve dramatically over the coming years.

Communication capabilities will also develop dramatically. For example, the GSM 5G standard is optimized for data rather than voice, and our phones will respond accordingly. A major area of development is in augmented reality; our phone will know more about where we are than we do and will share some of this information with us. As we enter a shopping mall, the coffee shop with a two-for-one offer will beep us, the bank will be alerted that we have arrived for our meeting, and our car will let us know when our three-hour free parking is expiring.

The corporate environment will use our phone's near-field communication (NFC) capabilities to open doors to restricted areas, multisite virtual meetings will be routine, and our devices will increasingly be used as control devices for the lights, room temperature, and presence indicators. Rooms will "switch on" when we enter them and "switch off" and return to a dormant state when we leave. Entering the dormant state will switch off the data projector, turn down the lights, close the window blinds, and turn down the heat or air conditioning.

Voice recognition will also become the norm. No longer will users activate applications via the screen, and they definitely won't be keying in passwords. Applications will respond to voice commands, and voice input will be used to record meetings—not audio but text. Voice recognition also impinges on identity management. It is now easy to authenticate a person by a voice print, and two-factor authentication using voice recognition is becoming commonplace.

Maturity Index

It is useful to periodically measure an organization's IdM maturity level and use it to construct a development roadmap to improve the identity and access management environment.

A Capability Maturity Model (CMM) framework is one such tool that is useful to evaluate an organization's current state and plan the migration to a higher level.

An organization's IDM environment can be mapped on a five-level maturity index, as shown in Figure 2.3.

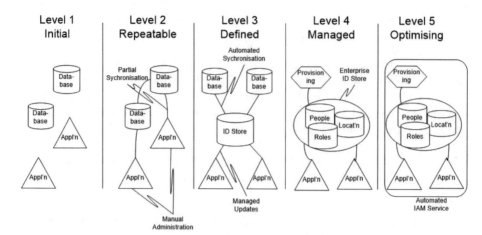

Figure 2.3: IDM maturity index

CMM1

This level is characterized by standalone applications, each maintaining its own identity data repositories. This means that the same identity data is entered multiple times and is held in multiple locations. This, in turn, means that when one piece of identity data changes in one application, it remains unchanged in another. This creates a data management overhead for both the data repository managers and the users who must accommodate out-of-date data.

CMM2

At level 2, multiple identity data repositories are maintained, but processes are established to ensure that when data is changed in one application, it is changed in "dependent" repositories. This level is reached over time; an organization achieves this level when the bulk of its data repositories are synchronized.

CMM3

Level 3 sees the establishment of processes to support the collection, storage, publication, and archival of identity data. This means that policies and procedures are in place and agreements are documented in regard to the definitive source of data attributes. Synchronization of databases is automated and consistent; that is, there is only one way to update an identity repository, and it is not vulnerable to process variances between system administrators.

> The zero-day requirement is sometimes not
> straightforward. During a recent assignment at a large
> Asian airline, the provisioning of pilots was brought up.
> The SAP record was activated on their first day of work,
> but the pilot roster was prepared a month in advance.
> Pilots who had recently joined the organization could not
> access their rosters online for their first month of work.

CMM4

Level 4 is characterized by the extension of the directory service into a managed service whereby identity information becomes more controlled. This is more easily achieved via a centralized directory service rather than a virtual directory service. At this level there is no identity data-repository update left to chance, and strict controls are enforced to ensure high accuracy and integrity of service.

CMM5

This optimal level is achieved only when the identity and access management facility is self-sustaining and its efficacy in accommodating organizational requirements is maximized. This means that self-servicing is maximized, workflow manages all authorization, and repository updating and de-provisioning occur upon cessation of duties for staff and contractors. Fast response to organizational change must be supported, and integration with audit facilities must be in place. Identity data repositories must be both current and accurate.

Conclusion

There is little doubt that "identity is the new perimeter." You can no longer rely on network devices to keep out nefarious users. The ability of an organization to manage identities and entities within its boundaries is not only a prerequisite for cybersecurity, but will increasingly be a competitive advantage, too.

Organizations must deploy identity and access management technology commensurate with their security requirements and need for business enablement. Security will be enhanced by a robust identity data store that can service access requests. Business enablement will be made possible by extending support to "things" and the new opportunities that are arising in the cloud age.

Getting IAM right is a prerequisite to prospering from, and not falling victim to, digital transformation.

Use Case: Contracto Building Contractors

Scenario	Contracto has three corporate applications that are accessed by all staff and two applications that are accessed by building staff, 80 percent of whom are contractors. Staff details are exported from the HR system every night, and the identity management system imports changes and writes the new records to an enterprise database. Contractors are managed by the finance department. Contracting companies provide a file of contractor details. An administrator in the finance department keys the data into a common database used by the two building applications.
Strategy	An audit of Contracto access management has identified deficiencies: administrative staff cannot access the building applications for basic reporting requirements, and the identity store for the building applications contains orphaned accounts with active access rights. Management wants to streamline the provisioning into corporate applications, clean up the identity data store, and raise governance over the management of identity information within the organization.
Solution	Contracto engaged a systems integrator to upgrade its enterprise directory and deploy an open source contractor management system. A federated authentication system was also deployed, supplying cross-domain federation. The directory was expanded to accommodate all contractor staff with an interface to the contractor management system. For authentication purposes, the larger contracting companies were integrated with the new federated authentication tool to automate the access for approved staff. This meant that, if a contractor left the employ of their contracting organization, they would no longer be able to log in to Contracto systems. Contracto estimates that these changes improved the maturity of their identity management environment from 1.5 to 3.0.

Q & A

Q. Given that IdM touches all applications in a company, how can managers of systems being provisioned manually determine whether their access control requirements could be accommodated by the IdM system?

A. This is a chronic problem in many organizations. IT departments work diligently to provide an identity management environment that is both effective and efficient. In most cases, the service is regularly updated to release new features and keep up with technology. Usually the HR department is made aware of new functionality and is ideally part of the team that implements product/service upgrades.

Unfortunately, system managers are often not involved in upgrades and are not made aware of IdM system functionality that they could potentially leverage.

This means that the organization does not optimize business efficiency and does not take advantage of functionality that can reduce their IT risk profile and potentially save the organization embarrassment and cost in the event of a preventable data loss.

At the very least, IdM system upgrades should be run as a project, and the identification of stakeholders should cast a wide net to allow business managers to monitor development activity and to get involved in project work that could, or should, affect their line of business.

For the project manager: it is suggested that business managers should attend stand-ups and be intimately involved in project development, testing, and release. It is highly recommended that upgrade projects be included in corporate communication facilities and that the project wall includes an appropriate communication task to make staff aware of the development.

Q. How should an organization decide the level of maturity that best suits its identity management circumstances?

A. This is typically related to size. The larger the organization, the greater benefit to be gained by improving the level of IdM maturity. It will also cost more to move up the maturity scale, so smaller organizations might find it prohibitive.

Generally speaking, any company with more than 1,000 identities should have some form of identity management system. Since most organizations at this level will be cloud-based, it is not difficult to establish an IDaaS offering that will service the company's main applications. For larger organizations that have both on-premises and cloud applications, as well as multiple types of on-premises apps (e.g., Web, client/server), implementing an IdM system is a little more complicated but should be firmly grounded in making the user experience as easy as possible. SSO across all on-premises systems and cloud applications should be a major goal. Federation with partner identity data stores should also be a goal. A policy should be established that new applications must be integrated, in some way, to the IdM infrastructure. At the least, integration should be via a mechanism such as AD groups (or another network directory). Preferably new applications should access the identity provider service, typically a directory, within the organization when determining access control for a user request. Ideally this should be via an external, policy-based authorization service.

The real requirement can be summarized as a need to raise the IdM environment to executive management level to ensure that it gets the right focus and high-level management attention.

Q. Who should determine approval workflows within an organization?

A. The business units. Access control entitlements provide users with "rights" within business unit systems. It is not the purview of IT to set these access rights, which often happens when IT relies on the access control settings of a peer when establishing entitlements for a new hire.

When workflows are initially deployed, a representative from each involved business unit should be engaged when configuring approval workflows. This representative will advise on access levels within relying applications and the approval required. Typically, an approval hierarchy will need to be established to control escalation of non-actioned approval requests.

It will often be necessary for the business unit representative to escalate decisions to upper management for policy determination. This is a good thing because it ensures corporate governance.

Chapter 3

Directory Identity Stores: Where Are They Now?

A core component of any identity management solution is a directory to store identity data.

By definition, an identity management solution stores people's identity data in a data repository such as a directory. Whether the information is staff records, business partner accounts, or customer details, it must be retained in order to manage people's interactions.

From a corporate perspective, most organizations need to store data for staff and contractors. Enterprise directories are typically used for this purpose. These directories are generally quite complex since they must service line-of-business applications and corporate requirements such as contact data, financial delegations, and workgroup memberships. Organizations need to know who is accessing their systems, and to be sure that they are allowed to do so. That means that in addition to biographic details such as name, address, date of birth, and gender, the directory must store organizational data such as department, manager, position details, and position number. In addition, the directory might also store biometric data such as fingerprints, or templates for finger or facial recognition. In many cases, these directories are hierarchical, so that they can represent the company's organizational structure.

Some organizations elect to use a database instead of a directory to store identity data. While this is usually adequate for smaller organizations, once a directory is large (more than 100,000 records), a directory typically provides better performance. For example, telecommunications companies (telcos) that require capacity for millions of records universally use directories for their identity data management.

Citizen directories are generally more simple. They have a flat structure since there is no need for the directory to store complex data attributes and hierarchical organizational data, but there is a need to store relationship detail. As we shall see, this requirement is defining the development of directory services for systems that cater to public access.

History

A quote often attributed to Winston Churchill is: "He who does not learn from history is doomed to repeat it." In the interest of understanding the present, in light of the past, here goes:

Not so long ago, identity management (IdM) was nicely compartmentalized and understandable. There were about a dozen vendors in the market, and defining a solution was relatively easy, once a company's size and propensity for an enterprise directory were known.

A common approach to providing a directory service was to establish an "enterprise directory" for all employees and contractors. As new staff joined the organization, an entry was created in the central directory that held identity information, contact data, and position details. This information was then used to provision into computer systems within the company and to set up email accounts and file share memberships. The authoritative source for most identity data was the HR system, with additional data such as phone numbers coming from an authoritative system such as the PABX. The directory was the source of truth for staff data: it drove the white pages application and, for sophisticated companies, the organizational charting function. Everyone was happy.

The first shock to this nirvana was Active Directory (AD). Microsoft significantly expanded its directory service to make it the ubiquitous directory service for authentication to network services, file shares, and Windows applications. Besides putting Novell Directory Services out of business, this strategic move by Microsoft caused confusion in directory services planning. Many organizations tried to migrate their enterprise directory to AD, but that never really worked. The use case for an enterprise directory is very different from the use case for an authentication directory. Enterprise directories should be very responsive to the business requirements, and administration should be done by the business units; if a new attribute is needed to store additional information, it should be easy to create it. Authentication directories, on the other hand, are mission-critical services with specialist system administrators who should be able veto any structural change.

The best implementations of a directory service were those that interfaced the enterprise directory to the authentication directory to provide a single environment with multiple functions. The enterprise directory maintained its "source of truth" status, adding new users to AD as they joined the organization and disabling their accounts in AD on exit from the company's employ.

The second shock occurred with the advent of cloud services. Suddenly it was necessary to throw out the old paradigm of a central directory and firewalls at the perimeter, and figure out how to avoid opening up the enterprise directory to the world. Legacy directory services were no longer appropriate since they normally used LDAP, not a suitable protocol to expose over the Internet, and they resided behind a firewall, inaccessible to cloud-based apps. In response to this restriction, most software as a service (SaaS) apps established their own identity stores, and many organizations started to synchronize their identity data to multiple locations on the Internet. While this was a pragmatic move for a company, it significantly raised the organization's risk profile, as each additional repository represented an attack vector for hackers.

So most organizations then faced the question as to how to service SaaS applications without either exposing their enterprise directory over the Internet or synchronizing identity data to multiple locations in the cloud. With the HR and IdM systems on the internal network and the SaaS applications on the Internet, some "magic" was needed. Fortunately, such "magic" is available, in the form of IdM solutions. Furthermore, most cloud providers now support an identity store in the cloud via the SAML protocol, integrating applications and cloud-based services.

Directory Use Cases

It's worth reviewing the basics of an organization's directory requirements and the requirements to be observed when constructing an identity store that must support a wide variety of functional requirements and application connectors.

Enterprise Directory

An enterprise directory is a business application that must be flexible enough to accommodate the needs of the corporate community. In an enterprise directory, if an additional attribute is required, or if there's an organizational structure change, there should be no constraints on how or when such updates can be made. Furthermore, the enterprise directory should be a rich source of staff contact details and should provide capabilities such as organizational charting.

Enterprise directories will typically have an LDAP interface for on-premises apps and a SAML interface for cloud apps and federation purposes. This means that the directory will need to support a hybrid[1] environment. The directory service

---

[1] *Hybrid* in this context refers to an environment that spans on-premises and cloud-based infrastructure/applications.

must maintain the referential integrity of the directory instances; that is, the synchronization between the on-premises and cloud-based instances should be a directory service function and not require regular involvement of a directory administrator.

Companies that use large enterprise directories to manage their staff and contractors need to maintain this repository both on-premises and in the cloud— that is, components will be kept in cloud storage synchronized from the on-premises instance. This is different from the authentication directory; typically, AD will remain the authentication source for the network, on-premises Windows apps, and print services, and the enterprise directory in the cloud will accommodate the authentication/authorization task for user's access to applications. This means cloud authentication services will require the directory to support modern protocols such as SAML or OAuth.

Microsoft Azure AD can provide this service, as can most cloud-based directory services.

Additional services for an enterprise directory include providing a white pages lookup facility and possibly a blue pages lookup for services. For example, the contact detail for the facilities manager at a particular company building should be locatable by both the person's name and their position.

The directory should support an organization chart facility to allow users to understand the reporting lines within the organization and to determine responsibilities and delegations.

Authentication Directory

An authentication directory is a mission-critical piece of infrastructure with administrators who, quite rightly, can overrule anyone making changes to it.

Authentication directories are typically provisioned from the HR system or via the enterprise directory system and are used to control access to corporate systems and applications.

The cloud has added confusion to the authentication task. We now have multiple applications in the cloud that need to access identity information to authenticate users. The typical solution has been to synchronize our identity information to each SaaS application that wants it. This results in a proliferation of identity stores in the cloud and represents a significant corporate risk: each additional cloud-based identity data store represents an increase in an organization's risk profile.

Microsoft realized this with the release, and rapid development, of Azure AD. The Azure environment, Microsoft's cloud solution, is anchored with the Azure AD directory. Initially this was synchronized with on-premises AD via the DirSync product, which moved a subset of identity information to the Azure environment. Now Microsoft's model is to make Azure AD the corporate repository and support legacy applications via a basic AD or via synchronization to Azure AD. The cloud has won.

Azure AD is significantly different from AD. Firstly, Azure AD is built on a graph database, which means it is well-prepared to accommodate the enterprise directory requirement to manage relationships. Secondly, it is equipped with an OData interface, which means it is better placed to perform sophisticated lookups via a Web services connection rather than a legacy directory that relies on LDAP/LDIF. Data can be passed in an encrypted and/or signed message using a JSON array rather than a flat file. Thirdly, because of its cloud infrastructure, multiple instances of the directory can be established to accommodate network latency issues for applications on a global basis.

Directory Trends

When planning an enterprise directory service, there are some obvious trends and some indomitable truths that you should be aware of to future-proof a directory deployment. Let's look at these trends.

LDAP

LDAP is not "dead." It will live on to service on-premises applications that already have an LDAP interface. It is still the "lowest common denominator" for a directory interface. Maintaining a capability in configuring LDAP filter lookups, and manipulating LDIF files, is recommended.

The trend is now toward support for a higher-order interface for high-volume directory queries. A likely contender is OData because it is a standard and it is supported by Microsoft.

> As part of work done with a health care organization, a survey was conducted with six large health care software vendors. One of the questions sought information on support for modern interface protocols. LDAP was the only common denominator in the responses.

Externalized Authentication

Application developers are increasingly externalizing access control decision-making and removing access control logic from their computer programs. Relying on an external decision point"—that is, moving from a coarse-grained authentication to a fine-grained authorization service—is the current trend. This trend is accelerating, particularly as customers increasingly support mobile devices and need better risk management applied to their access control decisions. As this occurs, a mature identity repository is required to support decision points and to act as the source of attribute data for access control policy evaluation (see chapter 4 for more information).

Cross-boundary Authentication

Monolithic directories are no longer satisfactory to service today's computing environment. They typically don't support SAML, the preferred protocol for cross-boundary authentication, and while they may be retained as a "source of truth" for on-premises applications, cloud applications and mobile devices will need access to a directory service that is readily accessible. This means that a cloud-based repository of at least some identity information will be required. For instance, a cloud-based financial accounting app only needs to be accessible from staff in the finance department. This means that the directory service of the future will be more fragmented and will likely be an amalgam of multiple, distributed identity stores that support a variety of access management models.

Modern Standards

For a basic UID lookup, programmers today want to use access methods that better suit their development environments. This typically means a Web services approach using an HTTP method. For situations in which higher security or greater throughput is required, a programming approach that involves accessing a RESTful API will typically be adopted. To pull back multiple data points, developers prefer to use JSON arrays. Ideally, meeting these needs will require an intelligent directory service that can accommodate data joins from multiple repositories and optimize lookup requests. The OData protocol is expected to become increasingly more important for developers of connectors between identity instances.

The use of standards for provisioning is becoming more important. There is increasing pressure for standards such as System for Cross-domain Identity Management (SCIM) to be supported by identity provider services, particularly if identity attributes must be periodically updated to multiple directory instances, each of which provides a component of the company's identity management environment. For situations in which SaaS apps must maintain an identity data repository, SCIM is the preferred protocol for the provisioning of identity data into a data repository.

Directory Design

Directories must be properly designed. It is not appropriate to purchase a vendor's directory solution and just populate it without determining the most appropriate schema, the number of instances, the distribution of data across the instances, and the appointing of appropriate administrators.

A directory is made up of *entries*, and against each entry there are *attributes*, sometimes called *properties*. Each person in a directory should only have one entry, and their pertinent attributes will be stored in that entry. Some attributes will be mandatory, in which case there will be a default value that can be changed—but it must be present. Some attributes will be multi-variable—that is, there can be several items in the attribute. One attribute will be an index (i.e., a unique value for each entry). This will typically be the person's employee number or assigned user ID. For directories/databases of large data sets of members of the public, an email address will often be used for index purposes.

The attributes to be stored against each record in the directory must be determined and documented. Each attribute should have a name that suggests its content. The inetOrgPerson "standard" provides a suggested schema for a person directory that an LDAP person directory can follow. The schema can be extended with additional attributes, but these should be appropriately named. The advantage of using such a standard is interoperability in the event that federation between organizations occurs.

> In one commercial organization, the AD admin proudly stated that the schema of their AD had never been altered: it used the standard structure and schema names. Unfortunately, over time, various individuals who needed to store data against persons in the directory had chosen any unused attribute and populated it with the information they wanted to store, regardless of the attribute name. This was not documented, and there was no governance over use of attributes within an entry.

Each attribute should have an authoritative source—where it comes from. Directories will often be designed to "write over" an attribute of an entry that does not conform to its authoritative source.

The index attribute should be selected carefully. In some cases, HR will not want the employee number used as an index because it might be deemed personally identifiable information (PII). Privacy regulation should also be observed; in many jurisdictions there are restrictions against using a government identifier, such as a driver's license, as an index for a directory. A separate system login ID is used in many companies, but the provisioning engine must be able to guarantee uniqueness when creating a new account. In a lifetime user ID situation, effort must be expended to ensure that returning staff are issued their original UID and not a new one.

Duplicate accounts can occur if the provisioning process does not guard against it. This problem can happen when a business unit computer system requires data for an identity that is not in the data store. In this instance, a new entry will be added. However, if this is not done correctly, a double entry might occur, and a reconciliation task will eventually be required to correct it.

> In a state government situation, an audit identified multiple staff with multiple IDs. It was not uncommon for a person to have four different login accounts. This caused many downstream problems as email accounts were assigned to the wrong UID and inconsistent access was given to file shares across the various accounts.

To guard against double entries, a provisioning system can be configured to generate an exception on a match of three or four attributes between a new entry and an existing record in the data store. This would then require a manual check before completion.

Synchronization vs. Replication

Synchronization is the copying of data from one location to another. This is often required if data must be copied between different data stores. It is an external activity that happens between separate directories. Synchronization is different from replication, which is an internal directory (or database) feature that copies data from one instance of the directory to another. Replication is typically used for performance purposes or redundancy reasons whereby multiple copies of the directory running on separate servers allows for more processes to respond to queries and provides resilience in the event of a server failure. Replication is most appropriate if a directory is geographically distributed and subsets of the directory reside in separate regions. Replication will ensure that referential integrity is maintained between instances of the directory service.

Data synchronization between the various data repositories within an enterprise is important because it's the only way to tie together the various account access entitlements a staff member might have in the organization's various systems. As noted in chapter 2, most large organizations are now using provisioning engines that integrate HR system entries with the authentication directory. Fewer organizations are leveraging the directory infrastructure for access control decisions. Those that do are typically using AD group memberships, for AD-aware applications, or they are providing an LDAP interface for real-time lookup during a login activity. But we now need to develop better access control using fine-grained authentication. The directory store needs to support more modern protocols, such as SAML and XACML (see chapter 4 for more detail).

PAM Solutions

Another consideration when developing a directory solution is privileged account management. In some cases, a system administrator will have two or more accounts: one user account with their UID and an account with privileges suffixed with Admin or AD. This is not ideal because AD admins need to remember which account they are using, and they should minimize the length of time they spend logged on with elevated privileges.

Some organizations have deployed a privileged account management (PAM) tool specifically to overcome this problem. Increasingly we are seeing alternative solutions whereby an account can be elevated to system administration privileges for a short, configurable period of time, after which it reverts to a normal user account. This can involve an approval request or notification to a manager for monitoring purposes. Azure AD Privileged Identity Management supports such a facility.

Directory Models

Planning a directory service is not a trivial matter; directories suffer from an "out of sight, out of mind" syndrome. When directories are working well, no one notices. It's only when they break that we realize how much we depend on them. It's often difficult to justify funds to develop a robust directory service to support the complexity of a modern IAM environment.

As with most technological environments, directory technology is never static; it is always moving and developing in accordance with user requirements. It is therefore important that we retain a competence within the company to plan and manage them.

There are three broad approaches to directory services that organizations can adopt. As an organization's IdM environment matures, it is likely that they will support each model as some point in time.

Classic Directories

Most large organizations maintain a legacy directory that supports contact data lookups and services an authentication directory for on-premises applications. Most Windows-based applications rely on Kerberos to support single sign-on (SSO), so a local AD is often mandated. Users are happy, enjoying SSO between their Windows apps. If a Web access management (WAM) product is deployed, SSO is extended to Web apps. Figure 3.1 illustrates this type of classic directory configuration.

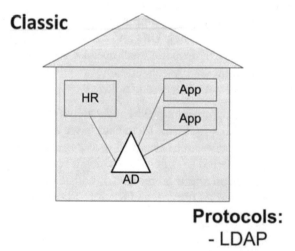

Figure 3.1: Classic directory configuration

Most WAM solutions rely on AD to provide a level of consistency across the application set. That is, AD becomes the common authentication directory for the organization.

In this environment, selecting a directory protocol is generally quite simple. LDAP is required, and organizations will maintain a competence on staff who can optimize a LDAP filter query. Large LDAP directories with multiple replicas can sometimes suffer from inconsistency between sites, but generally services built on LDAP directories serve their purpose well and are very efficient.

Hybrid Cloud

On-premises directory services are insufficient to support cloud-based applications. As more SaaS apps are engaged, LDAP is no longer appropriate. While a typical solution involved periodically sending identity data to various SaaS apps, usually on a nightly basis, this exposes organizations to unnecessary risk on two fronts: multiple instances of potentially sensitive user data are created in the cloud, and the nightly files sent to SaaS applications are often not encrypted because of the extra work of distributing encryption keys. Furthermore, many directory services do not support a delta file update, so full directory dumps are sent each night, which are then parsed by the SaaS applications to update their user repositories.

Instead of LDAP, SaaS applications are increasingly supporting various forms of SAML requests, so that queries and responses can be passed at a Web services level with either or both encryption and digital signing, as shown in Figure 3.2.

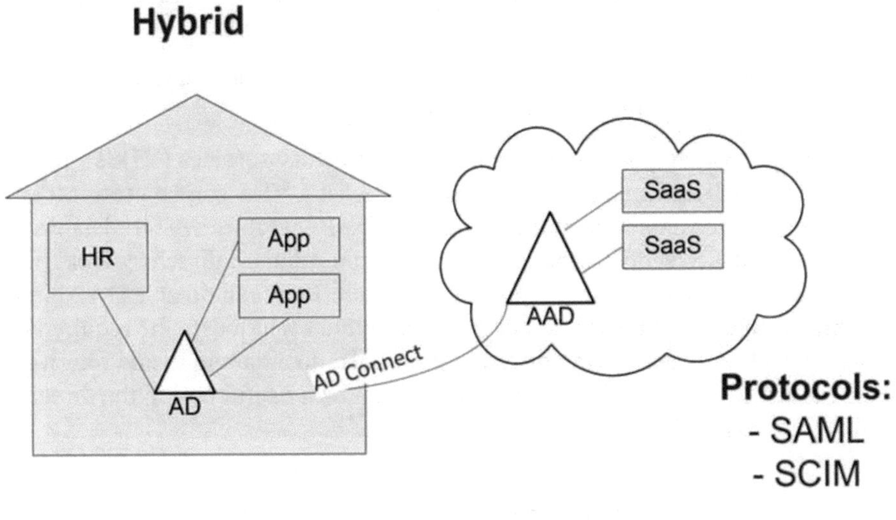

Figure 3.2: Hybrid directory configuration

However, a hybrid cloud environment has multiple challenges:

- Often on-premises directories do not support SAML.

- Permission is needed to get access to the directory through the firewall, although in most cases security rules will prevent this from happening.

- Network latency is an issue if the SAML request and response must transition the firewall and load balancer before the lookup can be passed to the directory.

For companies with a hybrid environment, it is important that an enterprise solution is mandated for any business unit wanting to engage a cloud service provider. All SaaS apps should be required to interface to the corporate in-cloud identity provider service rather than establish their own identity repositories.

Another option is for a SaaS provider to establish an identity as a service (IDaaS) implementation that is accessible by multiple apps (see chapter 5 for more detail).

Ideally a hybrid directory strategy should mandate a protocol standard, such as SAML, for cross-boundary authentication. Support for JSON and/or XML can be specified, and all requests should ideally be digitally signed (i.e., if a request is not from a known and approved source, it will not be actioned).

Furthermore, when establishing an in-cloud identity provider service, the standard protocol for directory provisioning is SCIM.

This is an appropriate point to mention virtual directory services (VDSs). In a situation in which multiple repositories of data exist a VDS can be useful. It sits between the source data repositories, be they LDAP directories, SQL databases, or Excel spreadsheets, and responds to queries in a standard directory lookup. For instance, an application might be just LDAP aware, so it can do an LDAP bind and send an LDAP get instruction to the VDS, which will locate the required data across multiple data sets, using different protocols, do a data join, and return a standards-based response. Virtual directories can be a useful tool in the directory administrator's arsenal.

Unified Environment

The future of directory services is a unified environment in which the location of data repositories is not important. In this environment, depicted in Figure 3.3, there is no real distinction between on-premises and in-cloud. The directory service must respond to a properly formatted authentication request regardless of where it comes from.

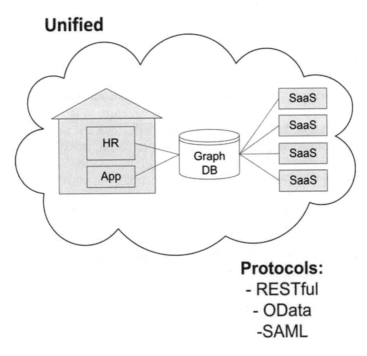

Figure 3.3: Unified directory configuration

Increasingly the direction is toward using graph databases instead of directories because of the databases' ability to manage relationships between entities and their ease of use for developers. There is no necessity to define a static schema, relationships between entities are easier to determine, and support for programmer APIs is provided. Programmers favor code that can be built into their software, such as SPAQL or Gremlin. The OData interface, behind a RESTful API, is gaining in popularity for writing to and reading from data stores.

It's also notable that the performance criteria for modern identity provider services have been relaxed in the cloud environment. No longer is subsecond response of an LDAP directory necessary; the Web services environment has some tolerance for network latency, such that database response in 2 to 3 seconds is usually considered adequate.

Consumer Directories

It was noted earlier in the chapter that consumer directories are a little different from enterprise directories. While much of our discussion has been about directories of staff, contractors, and business partners, it is worthwhile to consider directories of consumer data and recognize their differences from enterprise directories.

The major difference is scale. Whereas internal directory services typically deal with tens of thousands of entries, a consumer directory will need to accommodate hundreds of thousands, if not millions. Fortunately, in a consumer directory there is typically not a lot of data to store against each record. In fact, it's important to limit the information that is stored. In most jurisdictions, PII is protected through laws and regulations; thus minimizing the collection and storage of such data is highly recommended. This is particularly true of information such as credit card details. Typically, it's best to let the payment service store this information so as to not run afoul of Payment Card Industry (PCI) regulation and the potential reputational damage of a data loss (see chapter 11 for more detail).

Increasingly a consumer directory is being called upon to provide support for relationship information. This means a graph database is ideal for a consumer directory. It allows a less-structured storage of data with connections between "nodes" of attribute information. Searching a graph database allows the selection of the number of nodes to be searched which, in turn, controls the depth of information being retrieved (see chapter 10 for more detail).

Future Considerations

It's useful to consider the changes that are happening in the directory space to accommodate the changing directory requirements for cloud migration and consumerization. The main requirement is to establish a cloud-based directory to support access by members of the public to customer-facing applications.

Protocols such as SAML, OAuth, and SCIM should be supported, and for hybrid organizations there is a requirement for integration to their on-premises AD as well. The Microsoft Azure AD service provides this protocol support and facilitates this integration. For other cloud service providers, a synchronization from the organization's on-premises AD to the selected directory/data set in the cloud will be required.

Conclusion

In the brave new world of cloud applications, we no longer have the luxury of keeping a single, on-premises directory. We need a hybrid solution that unifies multiple data repositories and supports multiple interface protocols.

With so much focus today on new technology such as the cloud, mobile devices, and the Internet of Things, we typically don't want to be concerned about underlying technology such as directories. But the danger is that failing to properly manage the corporate identity repository endangers an important corporate asset.

An organization's directory service is firmly at the center of the enterprise architecture. It should be the "source of truth" for everything from names and addresses to biometric attributes and smartphone tokens. It must service the organization's cloud requirements and be able to accommodate relationship mapping between persons, devices, and things. It must support a variety of protocols such as SCIM and OpenID Connect and be able to parse JSON arrays and XML files.

This means that it must be planned, and policy must mandate its use. Relying parties should not be allowed to synchronize data. A SaaS app, unable to interface to the corporate directory, should be passed over.

The enterprise directory is no longer the monolithic beast of yesteryear. It's a much more diverse and distributed infrastructure that must provide an agile service that's central to the organization's security infrastructure.

Directory infrastructure is incredibly important to an IAM service. It is a core facility that will either make the environment work well, keeping users happy, or it will be a source of aggravation and potential vulnerability to the IT environment. Planning an organization's approach to directory services and ensuring that deployments are robust will be effort well spent.

Use Case: Telco

Scenario	Telco has a large directory of all residential and business customers in the country. The two sectors are separately managed with two separate directories. The residential directory maintains data for each subscriber against their address with a record of their plan, installation data, and expiry date. The business directory is more extensive, including details of the business ownership, industry sector, telephone service subscriptions, Yellow Pages advertising, and personnel who can authorize account decisions.
Strategy	Telco has no way of connecting business customers to residential customers. Various attempts have been made from time to time to undertake target marketing promotions to subscribers via an extract taken of residential customers with a match on name to the business database. Only 10% of business customers were matched with a residential account with an acceptable level of confidence. Marketing to this cohort converted residential mobiles to business plans at a 40% success rate, significantly reducing the chance of customer churn. It's now desired to centralize all accounts into a single directory infrastructure with the ability to provide significant relationship management and sophisticated big data analysis to track trends in marketing program success.
Solution	A NoSQL database was deployed, and both residential and business data sets were transferred to the new repository. A special one-off offer was made to business customers to transfer their mobile phone accounts to business accounts. The new directory was used to analyze business customers' geographic location and business sectors in order to deploy industry-specific target marketing for extended business telephone plans. For instance, it was possible to identify multi-sector businesses and extend their Yellow Pages advertising with inclusion in multiple local online directories.

Q & A

Q. If the need is only for cloud-based SaaS applications, should an organization establish its own directory service, or should it rely on an IDaaS from an organization such as Salesforce or Okta?

A. If the company has elected to use a service such as Okta, PingOne, or OneID, these should become the single source of truth for all SaaS apps—that is, those applications that are not "enrolled" in the service should be required to use the same IdP as the selected service. If a company is a Salesforce customer, it should consider using Salesforce as its identity provider service for cloud apps. If an organization currently does not use any cloud service that offers an identity provider service, the organization should deploy one and require all SaaS applications to use it. The intent is to limit the number of instances of identity data in the cloud.

Q. Why might you not want to maintain a data store of your customer information? What are the considerations when planning to do so?

A. While customer data stores are not as complex as staff or business partner data stores, they are an order of magnitude larger. They are also directly addressed in most jurisdictions by privacy legislation, which requires tight control on security and imposes constraints on how the data must be managed. There is therefore an argument that companies should rely on public IdPs. For instance, if all that's needed when a consumer visits your website is an email address so that you can send the visitor pertinent information about your products or services, relying on a public IdP would be a good idea. In this instance, you will provide a login box on your website that allows the visitor to use their GoogleID, Microsoft Live, or Facebook account to log in.

Q. What if data must be sourced from multiple locations (e.g., not just HR)?

A. This is usually the case.

Connectors are required to all authoritative data stores to be able to import the required attributes. Connectors should be configurable to update at an appropriate time (e.g., nightly), and they should be able to overwrite data that has been changed interactively; that is, if someone has manually changed a data element in the directory that has an authoritative source, it should be overwritten. Staff should be advised to always change data in the authoritative source rather than in the directory or downstream systems. This avoids inconsistency between data stores.

Another option is to employ a VDS to sit between the IdP and the provisioning tool, which "translates" directory requests into a normalized state. In this situation, the provisioning tool has one connector to the VDS, which then looks after updating the repositories behind it. All data lookups should then be to the VDS, which typically has data-join functionality that can construct sophisticated data lookups.

Chapter 4

Authentication and Authorization: Why?

Recent security and data breaches at a number of high-profile retail organizations and trusted providers of entertainment services have clearly indicated significant deficiencies in their access management infrastructure. In one instance, access to a contractor account, which had been provided for HVAC infrastructure monitoring, allowed hackers to access sensitive retail information. In another case, a system administrator account was maliciously used to cause significant data loss to the enterprise. Such incidents should not occur in this day and age because facilities to provide access control to meet any level of security exist and are relatively inexpensive.

Access control is the core of the identity and access management task. Once we have correctly provisioned user data into the enterprise's identity service, we can leverage it for access control. This leads us into the fascinating world of authentication and authorization.

Access Control Technology

Authentication and authorization refer to access control technologies. They allow us to manage who can get access to our computer systems, computer programs, and protected resources.

The line between the two functions is fuzzy, so we will start with the two ends of the authentication-authorization spectrum, shown in Figure 4.1.

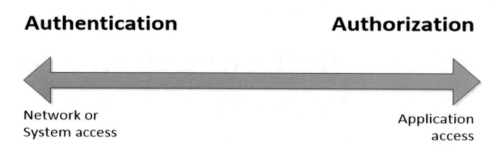

Figure 4.1: Access control spectrum

Authentication

Authentication is the act of confirming that a user is who they purport to be before granting them access to corporate resources. There are various ways to achieve this, but it usually entails a lookup on a directory service to determine the user's authority to access the requested service. A common use case is a network login process whereby a user enters their account name and password, the system then checks the directory service to see if the user has an active account and, if they do, provides access to the requested resource. In a Windows environment, once "logged in," a user will be granted access to any Windows resource on the network to which they are permitted access without having to "authenticate" individually for each requirement, provided Windows authentication has been enabled.

The term authentication is also used to describe access to a computer system—that is, system administrators "authenticate" to a server. This gives them access to operating system functions and the ability to manage the server.

Sometimes the term is used to describe the logon to an application, although this is now getting closer to "authorization." For instance, a user will sometimes be requested to "authenticate" to SharePoint, though in effect, the system is determining the user's access to one or more team sites within SharePoint. Thus, a more accurate description would be that the user is "authorized" to SharePoint.

Authentication Levels

It is important to understand levels of authentication. There is a vast difference between a Google ID or Facebook login and a secure corporate login via the company's identity management environment. The level of authentication will be determined by a risk analysis that evaluates "what can go wrong" if someone is inappropriately given access to an application.

The US National Institute of Standards and Technology (NIST)[1] provides guidance on the determination of the authentication mechanism for a desired level of assurance. A four-level model has been used for the past few years, but since most jurisdictions' privacy regulations mandate that anonymous or pseudonymous transactions must be supported, a five-level model is recommended, as shown in Figure 4.2.

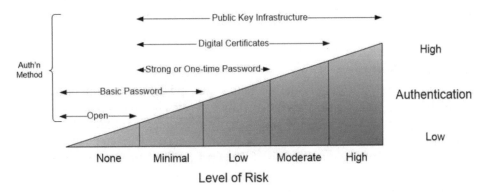

Figure 4.2: Levels of authentication

As the level of risk increases, the authentication strength must be increased.

Level 0 is for anonymous transactions where it is not necessary to identify the user (e.g., the purchase of theatre tickets). It might be necessary to collect a name for fulfillment of the transaction, but the customer should be free to choose a pseudonym if they want to.

Level 1 is for low-assurance logins. Many public access systems are at level 1. They access information and may require a contact, but there is no sensitive information to be accessed by the user. A basic username and password are satisfactory.

Level 2 is still for low-assurance logins but typically for corporate applications. Since there is little sensitive information to be accessed by the user, a username

---

[1] NIST 800-63 (2006) is the seminal electronic authentication framework document. This was superseded by 800-63-2 in 2013 to address cloud-based authentication and remote access. It is further updated by 800-63-3, which decouples authentication from identity proofing and specifically addresses federation.

and password will be required, and the company will typically impose a password policy that enforces a password of sufficient strength.

Level 3 is for medium-assurance applications where the user might be exposed to intellectual property of the organization or be able to access protected resources. In this instance, a higher-level authentication will be required, possibly protected by a biometric login or a digital certificate.

Level 4 is for high-assurance environments whereby significant damage could result if an incorrect authentication occurred. Industrial computer systems or military environments fit into this category. Public key infrastructure (PKI) or multi-factor authentication is appropriate.

Identity Proofing

Connecting a person's identity-defining attributes and the person him or herself is the identity proofing task. This is typically a non-trivial task depending of the level of registration required. For high-security environments at level 3, a substantial registration process will be required because the issuance of a certificate should not be made lightly if the certificate will be used to access sensitive, protected information. On the other hand, if it's simply to pay vehicle license fees, for example, a lower proofing level is satisfactory. Possibly this task could be outsourced to a public identity service by accepting social logins.

The steps then are:

1. User submits application for registration.
2. Uniqueness is verified, and proofing documentation checks are determined.
3. Identity-proofing documents are verified.
4. An identity assurance level is assigned.

Levels of Assurance

Determining the level of assurance involves a risk management approach based on an assessment of what could go wrong if a person accesses the target application fraudulently. In the event that serious consequences may occur, a high level of assurance should be assigned to the application. If consequences are slight or of no consequence, there's no point in engaging in a robust authentication process.

A typical evaluation process will be based on a four-level evaluation:

Low	Little confidence in the accuracy or legitimacy of a claimed identity Appropriate for transactions with minimal consequences to the organization or community from registration of a fraudulent identity
Medium	Some confidence in the claimed identity Appropriate for transactions where there may be low-level consequences if someone with a fraudulent identity is registered and accesses a service to which they are not eligible. Some minor consequences to the community may occur.
High	High confidence in the claimed identity Appropriate for transactions in which serious consequences could result from a fraudulent registration, such as inappropriate access to sensitive information or protected computer systems that could cause harm to the community
Very High	Very high confidence in the claimed identity Appropriate for transactions with very serious consequences associated with a fraudulent registration that has significant consequences to the community, such as the fraudulent issuance of a document commonly used as evidence of identity

Authorization

Once a user is authenticated, authorization provides access to computer programs (applications) commensurate with the user's authenticated identity. This typically involves a lookup of the user's record in the identity repository to determine their access rights within the requested application. There are several ways to achieve this.

Coarse-grained authorization is often achieved via AD groups. A number of AD groups will be established for an application, and the requesting user's AD group membership will determine the access they are granted in the application. For instance, if a user is in the Project Manager AD Group, the user will be authorized to the project management system as a manager. If a user is in one of the Project Team Member groups, he or she will be authorized to the appropriate project(s) at the user level.

Fine-grained authorization is completely different. It usually involves an authorization server that relies on a directory for attributes on users who request access to a protected resource, but it extends to a full dynamic attribute-based access control (ABAC) solution incorporating a decision point, one or more information points, and multiple enforcement points. The benefit that fine-grained authorization provides is the ability to establish centrally managed policies to provide governance over the authorization task.

This is a critical activity for any organization, but it becomes particularly important for a company with high-security requirements.

Access Control Types

Now it's time to change tack and consider authentication and authorization from another viewpoint. There are basically two approaches to enabling access control: a role-based approach that is usually used in the authentication task, and attribute-based access control that is the core of an authorization approach.

Authentication based on AD groups is a type of role-based access control. Users are provisioned into specific AD groups based on the workgroup in which they work or the department they belong to. In this way, they get access to systems and applications based on their "role" within the organization.

In an attribute-based access control system, shown in Figure 4.3, access is granted based on user attributes that are compared against policies that control who should get access to an application. The policy decision point (PDP) compares attributes that have been provisioned against a user in the identity repository, as well as context attributes such as the time of day, to determine the level of access a user should receive in the requested application.

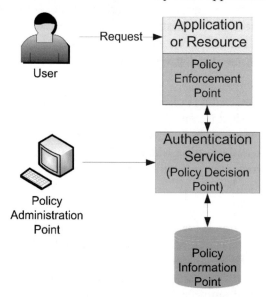

Figure 4.3: Attribute-based access control

Role-based Access Control

Role-based access control (RBAC) has served us well and remains a positive and efficient way in which to automate the granting of permissions to users, based on their roles in the organization. When a person joins an organization, their access to systems and protected resources in the organization should be commensurate with their role(s). Furthermore, when one or more of their roles change, their access to systems should change accordingly. For instance, if a person is a finance manager, they should have access to the financial management system at a manager level. If they then act as the chief finance officer (CFO) for two weeks while their manager is on vacation, they should be given access to the CEO meeting documentation for that period of time. If the manager is then transferred from Finance to HR, they should lose access to the Finance system and be given access to the HR system. This should happen automatically with human intervention limited to managing exceptions.

RBAC is therefore an efficient way to manage staff access to protected resources. RBAC becomes difficult, however, if there are too many roles. Over time, these lists become bloated and result in inherent risks to the organization. Often it is necessary for the organization to conduct a thorough assessment of the current assigned roles, which may lead to a consolidation and reduction of roles to those which are essential.

> In one state in Australia, the Department of Education found 1,500 different roles in schools across the state, making the deployment of RBAC difficult. The department analyzed the roles and distilled them down to eight. Each school was then required to assign their staff to one, or more, of the eight roles. Doing this significantly simplified the department's RBAC deployment, and the project was a success.

RBAC Example

Although there are many variants, all RBAC environments use a person's role information to grant access to applications. Let's look at an example, illustrated in Figure 4.4.

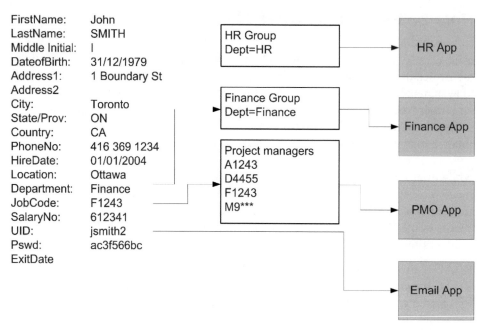

Figure 4.4: RBAC example

In Figure 4.4, John Smith is a Toronto-based staff member working in Ottawa. He gets access to the Finance application because he is in the Finance group. During provisioning, this group can be populated automatically from the Dept attribute in the organization's directory. The application's access control logic is configured to reference the appropriate groups when a user logs in.

In this instance, the project manager's group is configured for JobCode F1243, so John also gets access to the Project Management Office (PMO) application. This application's access control logic will perform a lookup on the corporate directory, when authenticating users, to retrieve the appropriate job code for the user in order to connect them to the application's functionality at the appropriate level.

Finally, John gets provisioned into the email program, as do all staff. Note: John does not get access to the HR application because he's not in the HR department. If he wants to access his HR record, he must contact someone in HR, unless the company has a self-service tool, with appropriate access control, to allow the user to access their record directly.

The Attribute Approach

In contrast to the RBAC example, attribute-based access control (ABAC) takes a very different approach to authorization. Access to protected resources is based on a user's having specific attributes—for example, name, date of birth, hire date, address, phone number, job title. This allows a much more fine-grained access control approach that combines not only user attributes but other data, such as location (IP address or GPS) and time of day, in the access control decision. It allows unprecedented control of access to restricted resources based on fine-grained attributes evaluated at runtime. Rather than just using the role of a user to decide whether or not to grant them access to a system or protected resource, ABAC can combine multiple attributes to make a context-aware decision in regard to individual requests for access.

Privacy Considerations

A rules-based approach to access control can leverage identity attributes to incorporate privacy requirements such as:

- Data minimization, where only personal data that is required for the provision of the requested product and service should be collected by an organization. It is not permissible to collect data that "might be" useful at some point in the future.

- Ensuring that anonymity is preserved if a person's identity is not needed for a transaction. It is only permissible to identity someone if doing so is required for the requested transaction.

- Restrictions on outsourcing personal data (e.g., several jurisdictions expressly prohibit personal data disclosure to a jurisdiction without similar privacy legislation)

- Enforcing use of personal data for only the express purpose for which it was collected and ensuring that any secondary purpose includes the collection of the individual's consent

- Ensuring government identifiers are not used for indexing

- Ensuring identity data is periodically updated to maintain its currency or is destroyed. If effort is not put into refreshing identity data on members of the public, in most jurisdictions it is illegal to keep this data.

ABAC holds significant promise for organizations that have a good identity management environment; it allows access to protected resources to be more fine-grained. That means that better overall security and improved data protection are achieved, and data governance is improved.

ABAC Example

There are various approaches to ABAC, but they all rely on a rich data store of attributes generally aggregated from multiple authoritative sources. The core principle is to adhere to a published policy that determines the attributes required to gain access to protected resources.

In the ABAC example shown in Figure 4.5, John will again get access to the finance application because he's in the finance department, but only on a view basis because that's all an F1** job code allows. He is also restricted to access during business hours. The access control system will allow him to access the PMO application but only the Ottawa projects.

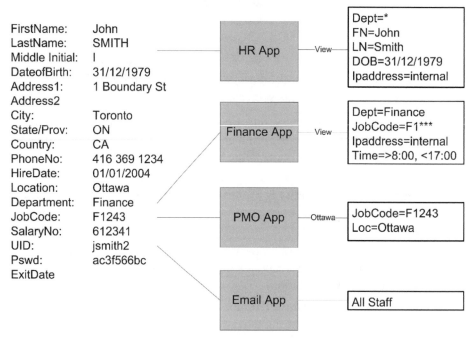

Figure 4.5: ABAC example

While John can't modify an HR system record, the use of ABAC supports a more fine-grained access to the application that allows him to view his own HR record. For HR staff, access can be segmented to roles; for example, if an HR person has a recruiting job function, they should get access to the recruiting subsystem; HR managers would get access as an administrator.

The benefits of an ABAC approach are significant:

- Access decisions are centrally managed via policies rather than by individual application managers. This means that they are consistent across the organization, and administered by business managers rather than controlled by IT personnel.

- Software development is simplified by the removal of access control logic and the incorporation of "policy enforcement point" code, which externalizes the access decision to a "policy decision point."

- Decisions are made at runtime based on attributes that can be combined to form fine-grained decisions; changes in access status are immediately recognized when attributes are updated.

From a business viewpoint, this means a vastly reduced risk profile; access rights will be modified as soon as the source system reflects the change. No longer will "old permissions" stay in the system when an attribute changes or a staff member leaves the organization's employ. Access rights are no longer based on access control lists that require manual intervention in order to be updated.

It also means lower costs: without manual intervention, there are no recurring costs for updating system access rights. Another benefit is that software development is less expensive because ABAC removes the cost of developing sophisticated access control logic from applications.

There are several considerations when moving to an attribute-based access control environment, and some challenges as well. First, a mature identity and access management environment is a prerequisite because ABAC requires a robust data model with predefined "authoritative sources" and efficient "source of truth" repositories for all attributes. Authentication is a mission-critical service; it must be highly available, and it cannot tolerate excessive network latency. This means that in some cases, a synchronization business model might be required whereby remote data stores are synchronized to a local directory or database.

Historical Note

It is useful to review the history of RBAC and ABAC.

Back in 1992, the US National Computer Security Conference issued a best practice document on RBAC, and in 1995 NIST issued an ITL bulletin indicating how RBAC should be implemented. The intent was to bring some commonality to the business processes associated with access control. These documents represent a seminal endorsement of the RBAC approach to access control.

In 2014 NIST issued SP-800 162 to provide best-practice guidelines for ABAC. The document provides a high-level view of ABAC and emphasizes the benefits associated with fine-grained access control. NIST has not endorsed any one ABAC protocol. While recognizing XACML as the most widely deployed protocol, NIST strongly supports what it calls Next Generation Access Control (NGAC) and has contributed to a functional architecture to support this approach, released as ANSI INCITS 499-2013.

APAM: An ABAC Implementation

ABAC has been with us for many years; it embodies a wide range of systems that control access to protected resources based on the attributes of the requesting party. As the field has developed, there are three characteristics that are most desirable in an ABAC system:

- It should externalize decision-making (i.e., not require applications to maintain their own access control logic).
- It should be adaptive (i.e., decisions are made in real time).
- It should be policy-based (i.e., access permissions should be determined based on evaluation of access control policies).
- It should be more than just control: business units become enabled to "manage" user's access control.

Adaptive policy-based access management (APAM) is a better term to describe a system that embodies these characteristics. It's adaptive because policies are evaluated at runtime, it's policy-based, and it's more than just access control: it's access management.

Attribute-based systems have several advantages: First, decisions are externalized to dedicated infrastructure that performs the policy evaluation. Decisions are also more fine-grained: if a user is a department manager, an APAM system can also check a user's department code and so decide, for instance, whether or not to give them access to the financial management system. It can check whether or not they are using their registered smartphone, and it can determine the time of day to make decisions that reduce the risk associated with an access request. Such systems are usually managed via a set of policies that allow business units to determine, for instance, whether or not they want to allow access from a smartphone, and if they do, to elevate the authorization level by using a two-factor mechanism.

The benefits are obvious: no longer are we dependent upon someone in IT to update an AD group, and more sophisticated decisions are possible. APAM systems are also real time. As soon as HR updates a person's position, their permissions are modified. The very next access request will be evaluated against the same policy set, but the new attributes may return a different decision.

The Configuration

To exploit the potential of APAM, it is necessary to augment one's IAM infrastructure to include a couple of additional items. Figure 4.6 shows a typical APAM configuration.

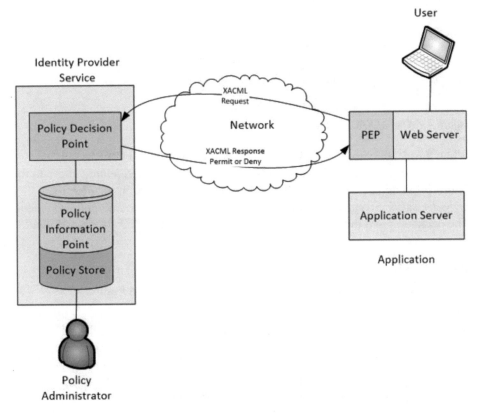

Figure 4.6: APAM configuration

The directory store migrates to an "information point," which provides the necessary data for the decision point to render a permit or deny decision. These decisions are interpreted by the enforcement point, a piece of code that sits on the Web server and controls access to the application in question.

The Query-Response Language

The heart of entitlements management is the eXtensible Access Control Markup Language (XACML) protocol. This standard has moved access control ahead immeasurably. It provides the process and technology for IAM environments to provide tight control over a wide range of resources. The use of XACML can be illustrated as shown in Figure 4.7.

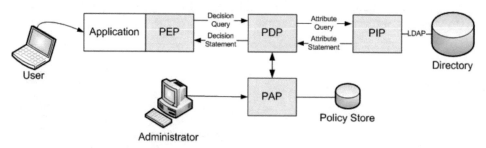

Figure 4.7: Use of XACML in an IAM environment

When a user accesses the application, the enforcement point (PEP) sends a *decision query* to the *decision point* (PDP), which sends an *attribute query* to the *information point* (PIP). The PIP looks up the user's record in the *identity provider service* (typically a directory) and responds with an *attribute statement*. The decision point then sends a *decision statement* to the PEP for enforcement.

Request

The structure of a request has four components, as shown in Figure 4.8.

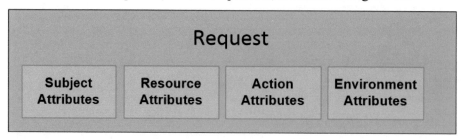

Figure 4.8: Structure of a request

The *subject* is the requesting entity. The *resource* is the application or documents to which the subject wants access. The *action* is the requested action, such as "view" or "write." The *environment attributes* are optional and can be used to specify other things such as time-of-day restrictions.

A request (simplified XML) might look something like the following:

```
<Request>
      <Subject>
            <AttributeValue>Alice@users.example.com</AttributeValue>
            <Attribute AttributeId="group"
             Issuer="admin@users.example.com">
      <AttributeValue>developers</AttributeValue>
      </Subject>
      <Resource>
            <AttributeValue>
            http://server.example.com/code/docs/developer-guide.html
      </AttributeValue>
      </Resource>
      <Action>
            <AttributeValue>read</AttributeValue>
      </Action>
</Request>
```

In this example, Alice, whose record in the directory indicates she is a developer, wants read access to the Developer Guide in the "docs" directory on the company's website.

Response

A response has three components, shown in Figure 4.9: the decision (hopefully *permit*), the status (should be OK), and any obligations on the decision (e.g., currency is in US dollars).

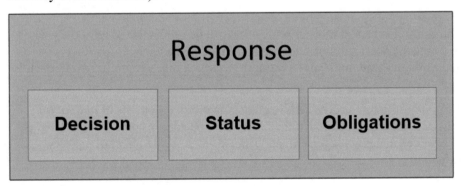

Figure 4.9: Components of a response

A *permit* response might look like the following:

```
<Response>
        <Result>
                <Decision>Permit</Decision>
                <Status>
                <StatusCode Value=":status:ok"/>
</Status>
        </Result>
</Response>
```

Other supported responses are: *deny* if the policy conditions are not met, *not applicable* if there is no appropriate policy, or *indeterminate* if there is insufficient information to make a decision, in which case more information may be requested.

Making Policies

One of the big benefits that entitlements management offers its users is the centralization of policies.

In most companies, policies are implemented in a haphazard fashion that is focused on individual applications. For instance, access policy for the Finance application is managed separately from the HR system, which is separate from the enterprise resource management system. This renders policy management costly and generally ineffective without a herculean manual effort to consolidate access control policy.

Centralizing policy management means that all business units with an application to be controlled can administer policy that can be implemented uniformly across the company. Most solutions have a distributed management capability to support multiple administrators, but it is important that a centralized approach is taken to ensure policy governance.

The policy structure in XACML is quite structured. It consists of *obligations*—that is, conditions under which the policy is to be administered, *target*—that is, the resource under management, and *rule(s)*—that is, the effect of a policy evaluation.

Policy administration, in support of an entitlements environment, is not to be entered into lightly. There are several points to note:

It is a business activity, not an IT responsibility.

It needs to be anchored in the organization's over-arching policy processes and procedures to ensure consistency.

It can be extremely complex unless managed by someone who can see the forest, rather than the trees.

In some industries (e.g., health care), there are already policy profiles that can be readily adopted by a new entitlements management system.

An Example

A policy might be established to allow the finance manager read access to the general ledger, accounts payable ledger, and accounts receivable ledger for the purpose of monitoring and reporting. In this case, the components of the policy are the following, also shown in Figure 4.10:

- Target—defines the applicability of a particular policy
- Subject—typically the entity that is the subject of the policy
- Resources—G/L, A/P ledger, and A/R ledger
- Action—read
- Environment—additional attributes to manage the scope of a policy target

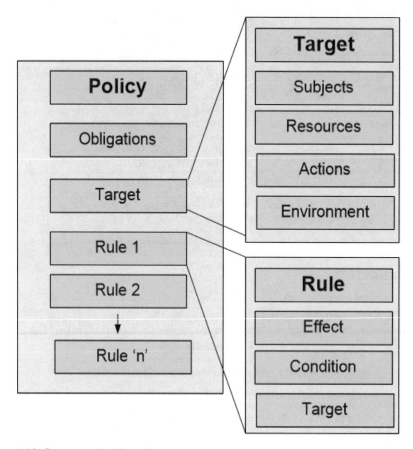

Figure 4.10: Components of a policy

There is an additional attribute set for policy purposes (e.g., monitoring and reporting).

Note: The policy administrator does not need to know how to format an XML file. The policy administration point (PAP) is equipped with a graphical user interface that generates XML code from English-language policy statements constructed with the help of pull-down menus.

Where to from Here?

So what's holding us back from deploying APAM systems? Firstly, there's the "if it's not broken, don't fix it" syndrome that encourages us to put up with less than optimal systems. Another detractor is the requirement for a mature identity management system in order to access attributes. There is also a need to manage policies: sometimes business groups are unwilling to take on the policy management task.

It's incumbent on C-level management to grapple with these issues. They must set the strategy and implement the requisite change management. If they do, not only will they be reducing the risk profile associated with their access control system, they'll open up new opportunities. It will be possible to more easily extend business system access to their business partners and potentially customers, for whom it is unsustainable to populate AD groups.

APAM has much to offer; we just need a willingness to embrace it.

Policy Management

A significant component of any ABAC environment is the requirement for a well-constructed policy management service. Most ABAC system vendors provide a policy administration manager (PAM) tool that facilitates the development and deployment of policies. There are several approaches to policy creation and management:

- The policy management console ships with predefined policies that can be configured to the organization's system specification.

- The policy administration tool provides a GUI with pull-down menus to build simple custom policies.

- The policy administration tool provides a natural-language, dialog-builder policy editor for the construction of complex policies.

- A programming interface is provided to facilitate construction of XML policies.

This is obviously an important differentiator between potential ABAC solutions, and it is directly related to the policy management approach that is to be adopted. If the business units within the business are to manage their own policies, the PAM must support a user-friendly approach; this will typically be a dialog-builder approach. If the company uses a policy administration unit staffed by specialists in policy management, a more technical approach can be adopted, and it is advisable that the unit have the capability to parse XML files.

Policy enforcement points can also be a challenge, particularly if there are many legacy applications to integrate. Old systems with built-in access control logic will need to be modified to externalize the authorization function and take advantage of the more fine-grained control that ABAC can provide. Vendors of

ABAC software assist this development by providing software development kits and API code that facilitate making legacy apps entitlement policy-aware.

Policy decision point management can be complicated for distributed organizations or hybrid situations in which some applications are in the cloud. While policy management must remain centralized, the decision points will need to be distributed, and a mechanism to keep them current will be required.

Finally, policy administration must be addressed. With the movement of policy management from IT to business, business units must understand their requirements and be able to encode their requirements in policies. In some organizations, this is hard to achieve, and a centralized policy management facility, servicing multiple business units, is required.

It is also recommended that a common foundation of terminology and concepts be adopted in order to encourage the greatest level of interoperability possible. Adopting a standard such as XACML is highly recommended, even though most XACML deployments contain a degree of proprietary logic. Adopting a standard can facilitate the integration of products from multiple vendors.

And Now a Word About Privileged Account Management

One of the major concerns for any identity and access management environment is how to control privileged accounts. Internal employees, or external contractors, are increasingly the source of threat within an organization. Recent hacking events at some very large organizations have been the result of either overt or surreptitious stealing of login details for privileged accounts. Such events highlight inappropriate procedures to thwart surreptitious approaches to staff and a lack of a risk-management strategy to adequately identify and manage internal staff threat vectors.

Privileged accounts are not normal user accounts. They have special permissions that allow a user logged on with one of these accounts to do specialist activities that are not available to the normal user. A system administrator account is a typical example. In order to manage a system, the administrator needs access to special functions that allow them to do dramatic things. A system administrator can typically access all files, even restricted ones, modify or remove users, and even shut down the system, if necessary. Such actions must necessarily be restricted to trusted staff, and access must be strictly controlled. A "four-eyes" policy[2] will normally be established that, at a minimum, will notify a manager that an account at administrator level has been accessed.

To this end, IT audits typically target the management of privileged accounts to ensure that there is proper governance over the granting of elevated privileges, the monitoring of special account management, and rescinding of privileges as soon as they are no longer required. Failed audits are a major driver for privileged identity management (PIM) system sales.

Types of Elevated Privilege Accounts

All systems have accounts with administrative privileges that normal users cannot access. These include standard system administrator accounts that can undertake special functions at the system level, such as turning on and off services, or the application level, such as adding or deleting users.

For UNIX systems, access at the root level provides access to all management features of the system, including CRUD (Create, Read, Update, Delete) permissions on the file structure.

There are also special accounts for database administrators. Such accounts can manage access to database elements, restricting access to rows, columns, or specific attributes. Tools are available now that will perform real-time redaction on data elements based on the attributes of a user accessing the database.

Principle of Least Privilege

The principle of least privilege states that at any point in time a user should have permissions at the lowest level of access they require to perform their job. Most users only need to access standard functionality, so a user's normal account should provide permissions only at this level. For instance, if your job requires you to be able to manage printers, your account permissions should allow you access to the printer administration function. Normal users do not need this functionality, so they should not be able to access printers at the management level.

An extension of this principle is very important for privileged accounts. The timeframe during which a user requires special privileges is actually quite small. Most of the time, a system administrator is not managing file shares, removing

---

[2] To counter potential corruption in granting access controls, a "four-eyes" policy may be adopted. Such a policy requires more than one person to authorize a user's access permissions to a sensitive resource.

users, and turning the system off and on; thus, most of the time, standard user permissions are quite satisfactory. The principle of least privilege will therefore suggest that system administrators' access at an "elevated" level should last for only as long as is necessary to perform the required activity; then the account permissions should revert to a normal user level.

An obvious benefit of such an arrangement is to reduce the incidence of inadvertent system administration activity. If the time a system administrator account is active is limited, the time available for mistakes or malicious activity is reduced. Least privilege also assists in forensic analysis. If accounts operating at an administrative level are minimized, it becomes easier to identify accounts that may have been compromised.

Types of Privileged Account Management

There are several mechanisms used to manage accounts with elevated privileges.

Note: The terms *privileged account management* (PAM) and *privileged identity management* (PIM) are often used interchangeably.

Password Vault

PAM systems become the gateway to the systems they protect. They typically comprise a password management facility that manages access to the protected resources. In effect, the PAM becomes the only way users can access the protected systems because they use complex passwords that would take an inordinately long time to crack with a brute-force attack.

PAM systems have the big advantage in that they provide a single location where privileged account passwords are managed. By taking a user out of the PAM system, their access is removed from all relying systems (other systems using complex passwords managed by the PAM system). A password vault system also provides a single sign-on (SSO) facility for users who have elevated privileges. Because the system is managing user accounts in the relying systems, once a user has authenticated to the PAM system, if they can click on the systems that are attached to their account, they can be automatically logged into the new requested system if the PAM has been configured to do so.

ERPM

Enterprise random password manager (ERPM) systems take the PAM operation to the next level. They monitor systems that have privileged accounts and periodically change the account passwords. They typically use a complex password to make any access outside the ERPM system difficult. One advantage of such as system is password rotation. If a management account is ever compromised, it won't be long until the password is changed.

Default System Password Replacement

A useful capability of some PAM products is the ability to prompt networked systems to identify and update any system that maintains a default password. Systems that have been installed without the default password being changed are automatically updated to a complex password and are then accessed via the PAM system. Though it may be hard to believe, many ransomware attacks have been enabled by systems being deployed without the default password being changed.

Pros and Cons of PAM Systems

Benefits

The main reason for installing a PAM system is to provide greater security to the granting of access to systems at a specialist functionality level. However, there are some added side benefits:

- Logging and monitoring of access to systems at a privileged level can be enabled. If a user remains online for extended periods of time, an alert can be raised and action taken. While this might not indicate nefarious activity, limiting access and returning users to a lower privileged account can minimize the opportunity for mistakes that might inadvertently cause business disruption.

- PAMs can be configured to automatically notify a manager whenever a privileged account has been accessed. This provides an extra level of monitoring that lessens the likelihood of privileged account abuse.

- PAMs can also be used to provide additional protection to relying systems. For instance, if system administration work is undertaken only in business hours, the PAM system can restrict access to elevated privilege accounts outside business hours.

Drawbacks

There are some issues to contend with when deploying a PAM system:

- Business continuity—centralizing account management in one system creates a business dependency on the system and, in fact, PAM systems become mission-critical infrastructure, for obvious reasons. If a PAM system experiences an outage, it is likely that access to other systems, at a privileged level, will be lost. It is therefore very important that PAM systems are built on high-availability or redundant systems and are adequately backed up. Backup data is also critical and must be adequately protected.

- Audit data—anyone wishing to subvert a system and remove audit trails of covert activity needs access to the system logs of the PAM system. It is therefore important to ensure that logs are adequately protected in a remote data store. Various technologies can be used to ensure that logs and audit reports remain tamper-proof. These might include storing logs on a protected subnet, the use of encryption, and/or requiring the use of electronic signatures for access.

- Assurance levels—as noted previously, system administration accounts require a high level of authentication, and PAMs give access to multiple systems at these elevated permission levels. If the PAM provides SSO for privileged users to access multiple systems, it is important that the selected authentication level for the PAM system matches the security level of the most stringent account access available from the system. For instance, an account requires strong password authentication for access to a mail system administrator account but also provides access to a medical records system requiring a smartcard certificate. The PAM system must require users to use their smartcard for access to the system, or prompt for a second factor if the user is not authenticated at the required level.

Strategic Approach to PAM

A PAM system acquisition should be approached from a strategic viewpoint that considers the wider implications of managing elevated privileges. Too often a PAM solution is acquired to provide a point solution for a specific problem. This obviates the benefit of comprehensive identity and access management. It is better to consider the management of elevated privileges as one component of a mature IdM environment and leverage the other components as part of this task.

Other aspects of an IdM environment that should be addressed in light of the PAM requirement are:

- SSO—does the PAM solution allow system administration personnel SSO? If there is an SSO solution in place within an organization, what are the rules for including PAM-controlled accounts in the SSO environment?

- Security information and event management (SIEM)—does the PAM system need to communicate with the SIEM system? If the organization uses a SIEM system, is there a need for visibility on out-of-band system administration usage? Any abnormal privileged account usage would normally be visible in the PAM system; the PAM system should also notify the organization's monitoring and audit facilities of such events.

- Identity federation—in some cases, privileged account access must be given to external contractors. For example, a common requirement is for a heating and air-conditioning contractor to have access to a building control system. In this instance, it is important for the system to be part of an identity federation environment that avoids the use of a generic account for the contractor but at the same time does not require the organization to maintain contractor accounts in its identity management system.

A strategic approach treats the PAM requirement as part of a holistic solution for an organization's identity and access management task. Privileged accounts are but one aspect of the provisioning and access control task. Many IdM solution vendors have a solution for privileged accounts that is integrated with the identity management system. Thus an organization's PAM requirement should ideally be added to the system requirements list for the IdM environment and not treated in isolation.

Bottom Line

A PAM system is an important component of an organization's security and data loss prevention solution. PAMs often represents "low-hanging fruit" when it comes to delivering a quick and effective solution to the protection of accounts with elevated permissions. But PAM systems should be part of the organization's strategic approach to identity and access management and not a "quick fix" as a result of an audit failure.

Conclusion

Access control is the target of IAM environments. There's no one-size-fits-all because each organization is on its own trajectory from basic authentication to role-based authentication and may or may not have an application for authorization. Organizations must develop their own approach to role-based systems and determine how to provision into target applications. Options range from the use of AD groups to setting entitlements directly into target system databases.

For organizations that adopt ABAC systems, the ability to modify legacy systems for policy enforcement and develop a policy administration capability is important.

Use Case: StateGov

Scenario	A state government conducted a review of agency requirements and found that most departments were adding external identities to the government directory in order to give commercial service providers access to departmental systems. It was identified that this was a major source of annoyance for the departments. It was also identified that there were security holes that was raising the risk profile of StateGov.
Strategy	The Department of Transport added certified vehicle safety technicians from over 250 companies to allow them to file roadworthy certificates with the department. This took one full-time employee to maintain. The Health Department was maintaining the user accounts of 75 radiologists who provided services in the state's five main hospitals and 55 clinics. The Family Services Department outsourced social worker activity to four service companies. Due to the churn within this cohort of contractors, generic accounts were used for each company to allow their staff access to the case note files.
Solution	A federated solution was deployed for the Health and Family Services departments whereby reviews of the registration processes of the radiology companies and the social worker organizations were conducted. On the basis of these reviews, a federated authentication service was deployed, which sent a SAML request to the respective organization's identity provider service when a user requested a login. The resultant SAML assertion was then used to connect the user to the appropriate service. For the automobile service centers, user accounts were maintained in StateGov's directory, but a self-service process was initiated with an approval cycle to the director of vehicle safety for authorization of each new person added.

Q & A

Q. Is ABAC a natural progression from RBAC?

A. No. ABAC is a different approach from RBAC. A mature RBAC environment, whether it provisions in AD groups or directly into relying applications, will satisfy most organizations and should only be replaced by an ABAC deployment if there is a need for:

- A more fine-grained authorization environment that evaluates multiple attributes, including context attributes such as time of day or geo-positioning
- Better governance with centralized policy administration to harmonize policy across multiple applications
- Reduced software development costs by externalizing decision-making, and removing access control logic from computer programs

It is expected that more fine-grained attribute-based access control will be adopted by specific industry sectors. For instance, health care could significantly improve access to medical applications with an ABAC installation that checks a health professional's credentials to operate a machine before giving access, or checks the hospital's roster before allowing access to an OT application.

Q. Should an ABAC system be XACML based?

A. Not necessarily. While XACML is arguably the most sophisticated ABAC protocol, there are other options. In fact, NIST strongly supports a Next Generation Access Control model (refer SP-800-162). XACML does, however, provide a complete framework, defining communication protocols between the decision point and the policy information point as well as the request-response messages between an application's PEP and the decision point. This means that, in a fully compliant deployment, components of the system should be easily swapped out and replaced by components from other suppliers.

It is noted that there are some variants of XACML. For instance, while the XACML protocol is XML-based, due to market pressure, a JSON variant is supported, which allows data between the enforcement point and decision point to be communicated in JSON arrays.

It's also important to realize that not all XACML system are fully compliant, with system suppliers often developing proprietary extensions for specific purposes.

Q. When is a standalone PAM system indicated rather than using the organization's identity management system?

A. PAMs are often installed after an audit failure or a data breach as a result of a compromised privileged account. Installing a PAM will immediately fix the problem and provide a level of governance over the management of accounts with elevated privileges.

Ideally a strategic view of account management should be taken, which includes the need for management of system administration and service accounts in the organization's access control policy and procedures. Often PAMs are deployed after an audit that identifies that there are too many privileged accounts and/or orphaned accounts with elevated privileges that have never been disabled. This does not indicate a need for a PAM; rather, it indicates poor identity management practices that need to be rectified.

Chapter 5

Then the Cloud Happened

Most companies do not plan their migration to the cloud. Perhaps as a result of a question by upper management, they find out one day that they have multiple users of cloud services in their organization. While each application was a good idea at the time, such a disparate approach means that there is no strategic vision, uncoordinated service provision, a significant training cost, and little governance over cloud-based applications and infrastructure.

The adoption of cloud services often starts with a software development group, or the team responsible for release management. Cloud services are indeed a boon to software testing. They make it so easy to spin up multiple instances of your application and undertake serious performance testing without requesting a server farm from the IT department, which would likely get turned down or take too long to get approved. All you need is a credit card and your supervisor's approval to submit an expense claim—it's a no-brainer.

Enough has been written about the cloud, some of it helpful, but a lot misleading or purposefully obtuse. Some vendors, it appears, want to make things complex so that confused customers feel that they have to engage the vendor to make sense of it. This is unfortunate because it can lead some businesses to make mistakes and expose their organizations to heightened risks. In terms of managing risk, there are some useful models that will assist businesses to ask the right questions of cloud service providers.

Three broad categories of risk must be evaluated when considering migration to the cloud: organizational risks such as loss of governance or lock-in, technical risks such as isolation failure or malicious insider abuse, and legal risks such as data protection regulation or subpoena processes.

So what's important from an identity and access management perspective?

First, understanding how the cloud elevates identity to an unprecedented level of importance. In the past, a typical approach to the cloud has been to try to layer on top of it a security model that better fits an on-premises environment. This is understandable because it is typically network specialists that are advising on system configuration for managed services. In other words, they are trying to duplicate the corporate network in the cloud environment. There are two outcomes: the resultant environment fails to take advantage of the cloud's inherent capabilities, and costs are greater than they need to be.

For instance, a tried-and-true approach to security in an on-premises environment is to segment the network into separate virtual LANs via switches that are programmed to only allow authorized traffic to secure areas. In this way, systems with similar access control requirements can be grouped on a LAN segment with reliance on the switch to restrict access only to authorized persons. To establish a similar environment in the cloud is expensive. A better solution is to use the inherent security enabled by the cloud services provider (CSP) and rely on them, as the managed service provider, to do what you're paying them to do.

Second, when approaching the cloud, many organizations seem to be "throwing out the baby with the bath water." They fail to implement the same level of protection they have on-premises when they move an application to a CSP, and they fail to implement features that users have come to enjoy, such as single-sign-on (SSO), when they move to the cloud.

> An Asian airline instituted a policy that no cloud services would be engaged because they could not meet the company's standards. In particular, physical access control to the data center and operational standards were indicated as issues that would disqualify a CSP from accommodating the airline's business. An audit of the data center operations revealed several severe contraventions of physical access control policy at the data center and multiple operational defects, such as failed disks in striped sets and no testing of power failover for high-availability systems—all situations that would not be tolerated by a cloud service provider.

Over time, most companies have developed well-thought-out approaches to their security requirements and have a model that matches the assurance level they need—that is, organizations with highly sensitive information to protect have robust access controls commensurate with their requirements. Organizations with a lower protection requirement will adopt a model with laxer access control requirements. Companies typically acquire commercial products that implement a security model that meets the protection required by their business groups. However, in some companies, workgroups or business units are allowed to adopt cloud-based applications that don't meet these requirements and don't ensure that governance practices are adequately observed. Generally speaking, the same practices instilled in the on-premises environment should be adopted in the cloud environment. This includes requiring all system access to authenticate to the corporate identity provider service (IdP). Organizations must therefore provide cloud access to their IdP, which is a typical shortcoming of the identity management approach of many companies.

A common solution to supporting applications in the cloud is to synchronize identity data to the application in question on a periodic basis. But each such instance increases the company's risk profile by putting sensitive data about the company's staff and business partners into the cloud, unnecessarily exposing it to potential release should the CSPs infrastructure be compromised. Although a cloud instance in itself is not the security concern, multiple identity repositories in the cloud are. This practice also perpetuates an archaic approach to identity management by maintaining a static data repository of identity data for access control to applications that is only periodically updated. If, for example, a staff member leaves the company, they will not be removed from accessing applications to which they had access until the next update occurs

So what should our approach be? First, we need to understand the various types of cloud services.

Cloud Services Overview

Cloud services can be categorized into four areas, shown in Table 5.1.

Table 5.1: Cloud services

Service	Description
Compute services	CSPs let you "dial up" the level of service you need. After selecting the desired operating system and configuring it for memory-intensive or compute-intensive requirements, you select the size and number of virtual machines (VMs) you want, monitoring them and adjusting them as necessary, with the billing reflecting your selections. Standard offerings include features such as auto-scaling of servers and load balancing between servers. However, if you don't want elevated charges from higher than expected usage, you can limit these features. Compute services are a major attraction to organizations with a "lumpy" workload that varies in compute-intensity requirements. They remove the necessity to provision for the high-use periods with equipment sitting idle at other times. Compute services are also most useful for software release management, where it's necessary to maintain multiple environments for development, testing, and production. Support for testing, where volume testing requires significant compute power, is an important cloud services benefit.
Storage	One of the major advantages of the cloud is the support for corporate storage requirements. Virtually any type of storage is now supported: • Tables, whereby any key-value type of data can be stored in massively scalable cloud storage that expands as required • Blob storage, providing basic disk-based storage for cloud applications • Files, providing standard Windows file APIs for cloud VMs • SQL database, which provides high-performance relational database operation in the cloud; the service is available on a tiered pricing model. Other benefits include robust business continuity services with data backed up in real time and securely stored in remote data centers.
Web services	Most cloud platforms have a rich and comprehensive website offering. Deploying a website is simplified, with the main content management services from Joomla to Drupal typically supported. In addition, cloud offerings include support for databases such as MySQL or MongoDB.
Ancillary services	Collaboration tools for work teams are often provided with support for secure data sharing and concurrent editing of documents. Some tools facilitate instant messaging (IM) and online meetings.

	Big data analysis: most CSPs provide Hadoop services and map-reduce functionality that allows big data analysis for semi-structured data. Message queuing services, API management services, streaming media services, scheduler services, and notification services can all be accessed to support your cloud. Two-factor authentication services: you can establish authentication polices for cloud-based applications that mix single-factor with dual-factor requirements. If users are accessing a corporate application from an external location, a one-time-password login via the user's smartphone may be required. The Microsoft Azure environment also supports a Windows Device Registration Service to facilitate multi-factor authentication.

Types of Cloud Services

The identity and access management approach in the cloud must fit the selected environment. There are many approaches to migration to the cloud, and each organization must determine the approach that suits it best. While there are many variants, there are basically three types of cloud services, described next.

Software as a Service (SaaS)

The main focus when it comes to the cloud must be on computer programs, or applications, that provide the business functionality an organization requires. These applications need to control who can access them, and they will rely on an identity provider service to "authenticate" users. Organizations that use a cloud-based application basically have two choices: ensure that they provide an interface to the corporate identity repository, or synchronize their data to the SaaS application and store identity information in the cloud. The former is obviously preferable because it is more secure and enables the organization to maintain control over the identity data repository. With the second option, the problem is data proliferation: you soon have many copies of your identity in the cloud, each of which increases the attack surface in the event hackers target your corporate identities.

The challenge, which we will address shortly, is how to support applications in the cloud when the corporate identity repository is typically on-premises.

Platform as a Service (PaaS)

A PaaS provider is a cloud service provider that makes a complete platform available upon which to operate corporate applications. This can be very advantageous if the requirement is to cease maintaining company-owned systems but the organization is happy to manage its own application environment. In this case, there is no dependence on an identity provider managed by the cloud service provider. Corporate staff will operate the identity provider service to satisfy application requirements. While the CSP provides security for the service, protecting it from external threats to the best of its ability, maintaining control over and protecting identity data remains a corporate function. This is a low-risk situation because there is typically only one identity repository. For SaaS apps outside the corporate environment, authentication should be to the company's cloud-based IdP, via an appropriate protocol.

Infrastructure as a Service (IaaS)

Like PaaS providers, IaaS cloud service providers are of little concern in regard to identity provider services. Clients simply buy the amount of processing power and storage they need, and the required associated services, such as a disaster recovery program. Clients are then responsible for managing their applications— including the corporate identity provider service—on this infrastructure. A problem can arise when multiple IaaS providers are engaged and multiple IdPs are established. The "cloud solution architecture" should discourage such an instance unless a different CSP is selected for a specific, and bounded, requirement (e.g., software testing, big data analysis).

Some CSPs provide what they call an IDentity as a Service (IDaaS) as a multi-tenanted managed service—that is, multiple customers use the same infrastructure. This may or may not be a good thing depending on your cloud strategy. If it leads to a single IdP for all cloud-based apps, it could be a good approach to solving the cloud IdP challenge.

When CSPs refer to managing identities in the cloud, they are typically referring to managing access for administrators of their cloud-based services—for example, database administrators, system administrators, or security managers. While this is very important, it is a different aspect of identity management since only a few administrators will need elevated privileges to cloud-based systems. For these accounts, there is typically a need for greater granularity on system access than for on-premises infrastructure: the system administrator who configures the number of servers, and the associated automated scaling, should probably not be the same administrator responsible for the management of database keys.

But the identity management task, which is our prime consideration here, is the large number of identities that must be managed for access to our protected resources, whether on-premises or in the cloud. This data must be kept safe from inadvertent release on the Internet, and it is important that organizations be able to identify the specific activities they have initiated in this area. Governance processes should periodically review these activities and verify that they are adequate and meet corporate guidelines.

Public, Private, or Hybrid

After the choice of cloud service type has been made, the next step is to select a service provider. Public cloud providers are generally the least expensive because they leverage their investment in infrastructure across multiple clients and ensure sufficient isolation between various client instances on the common infrastructure. Clients typically aren't concerned how the CSP achieves this and rely on the service supplier to ensure that data and applications are adequately protected.

Private services are provided by CSPs that deploy infrastructure for the exclusive use of a particular client. These are typically IaaS installations that suit companies that want to maintain their own applications. The CSP supplies and manages the equipment, and maybe the server operating systems, ensuring they are appropriately patched, but that is all.

Hybrid services can refer to a mix of cloud services but more typically refer to organizations maintaining an on-premises infrastructure as well as engaging a cloud service; the two must work together. This is popular with organizations that have a sizable investment in a particular supplier's equipment and engage the same vendor's managed service offering for new requirements, thereby saving on the capital expense of purchasing new equipment. This can be a good way to migrate to the cloud because applications can be ported to the cloud environment gradually. The common nature of the infrastructure minimizes potential operating system and storage device incompatibility.

Identity in the Cloud

When it comes to supporting cloud services with identity data, two main questions must be answered: what data repository should we use, and what interfaces are required?

Data Repository

The choice of a data repository will be guided by the required environment. This includes factors such as the predominant supplier for on-premises systems. If an organization is primarily a Microsoft environment, the cloud service environment will likely be Azure. If it's predominantly a Linux environment, an Amazon Web Services (AWS) or Google environment might be preferred. Table 5.2 lists some common cloud environments.

Table 5.2: Cloud environments

Cloud Environment	Description
Microsoft Azure	If an organization maintains a predominantly Microsoft environment, there would need to be a good reason not to deploy an Azure AD environment. Azure AD integrates well with on-premises AD infrastructure, supports all the required protocols, and will provide a degree of "future proofing." Azure AD is built on a graph database, so it can well accommodate relationship data, which is becoming increasingly important in the identity management space. Finally, the Azure environment supports all the main interface protocols.
AWS Solutions	If an organization has already adopted a SaaS solution provider such as Okta, OneLogin, or PingOne, the cloud IdP solution is already in place. It is most important that any new SaaS app that is engaged should use the existing IdP service, even if the application is not being enrolled in the SaaS solution. For instance, if an organization is a Salesforce customer, consideration should be given to using the Salesforce IdP service for all cloud apps. Regardless of which option is selected, it is important that organizations retain control of their identity repository in the cloud. Additionally, the organization should consider not engaging any SaaS apps that do not support a central identity provider service model.
Google Solutions	If an organization is a Google customer that uses Gmail, Google Docs, and other Google services, the obvious identity management solution is to use Google's identity and access management service to the degree possible (note: this is not the Google ID public IdP service). Organizations would still undertake their same registration processes but then store the

	data in their Google cloud service. The benefit is the well-managed API that Google maintains. Support for Google Groups, wide protocol support, and support for SaaS providers such as Okta, OneLogin, or PingOne, is provided.
Private cloud	There are a number of vendors that provide IDaaS services. For instance, an HP customer might engage the HP Enterprise cloud environment, a Dell customer might choose the Dell Cloud Computing Service, or an IBM customer might migrate to IBM cloud services. But once a cloud-based IdP has been deployed, integration with the organization's identity service should be a prerequisite for selection of a SaaS app.

Developing a Cloud Strategy

As with most IT deployments, it is important to set the strategy for the company before engaging a CSP. There are several components to this, each of which will affect the company's approach to identity and access management.

Policy

If there is one shortcoming in the deployment of many cloud services, it is in the policy area. In many cases, company boards of management are abrogating their corporate responsibilities by not mandating policy in the deployment of their information technology. Too often important decisions are being put in the "too hard" basket or ignored because the board members don't understand the ramifications. It is important for the CIO to understand the technology and not rely on IT staff to make decisions that, in effect, set corporate policy. The "don't tell me so I can't be blamed" approach is not tenable because of the risk of getting corporations into unnecessary strife. In fact, business schools should teach IT basics to business managers to equip them to ask the right questions and evaluate the risks associated with the main approaches to technology deployments.

It's highly recommended that an *enterprise architecture* approach be taken (see the Enterprise Architecture section on page 102). The cloud environment should be subjected to the same rigor that governs the on-premises environment. At the technical level, the operating systems and currently supported versions should be dictated. At the application level, the cloud-based programs should be included in the organization's application portfolio, along with the on-premises programs. At the information architecture level, entity relationship diagrams should map the data being passed to and from cloud applications and databases in the same way that on-premises applications are documented. The way in which the organization's IdP interfaces to applications should be included in the enterprise architecture documentation. At the business system architecture level, the focus should be on how cloud-based apps support business systems within the organization, ensuring that the performance of cloud apps meets business unit expectations.

Organizational Capability

A fundamental requirement in any strategy development is understanding the organization's capability. If the capability to implement a strategy doesn't exist, or is insufficient, it must either be developed or the strategy changed. As a simplistic example: if a company does not have the technical skills to manage servers and deploy applications, an IaaS solution is not a good idea.

When it comes to identity management, an organization can outsource the management of the IdM infrastructure but cannot outsource the responsibility for it. Regardless of the deployment model selected, it is the company's responsibility to ensure that it meets regulatory requirements.

User Requirements

It is equally necessary to understand user requirements, and it is here that many organizations are found wanting. IT departments are notoriously bad at getting close to the business units and working with them to design solutions that suit the business. But doing so is mandatory in order to deploy an efficient and effective cloud-based service. To fail to do this will mean that business units will seek out or develop solutions on their own, which will circumvent corporate governance processes and could result in the organization being exposed to unnecessary risk.

A better solution is for the IT department to facilitate connections to SaaS applications, to ensure that an optimal solution architecture is developed and that business functionality is provided within corporate governance guidelines. While business units tend to balk at the cost of governance processes, adhering to governance policy will normally be the least expensive option in the long term.

Data Storage Considerations

There are multiple policy areas that will impinge on storing data in the cloud. Companies must understand that controls are required for the data they will be collecting or retaining. Table 5.3 lists commonly used data controls.

Table 5.3: Controls for storing data in the cloud

Control	Description
Personally Identifiable Information (PII)	Most jurisdictions have some sort of privacy legislation in place. Some countries such as the European Union, Singapore, Australia, and Hong Kong have stringent laws in place that dictate how identity data is to be treated and limit the ways in which it can be stored. Adhering to these requirements will ensure adequate protection of identity data and will avoid wasting money on litigation defense.
Payment Card Industry (PCI)	There are now stringent rules on the storage of credit card and banking information on staff and customers. Storage of this sensitive information requires adherence to these rules, and audits need to be performed. It is generally better to not store such information if not necessary. For instance, if transactions are typically infrequent, capturing credit card details to improve users' experience entails more risk than is warranted.
Corporate-controlled information	Determining the classification of corporate data that can be stored in the cloud is a prerequisite for migrating to the cloud. Doing so will allow the proper determination of other types of cloud services to be engaged and what service level agreements (SLAs) are required. Corporate-controlled information typically includes documents that must be shared for board-level meetings, upper management meeting minutes, product development data, project team documents, production data, and HR information.

Selecting a CSP

To illustrate the issues to be addressed when selecting a CSP, we will use the market leaders in the public cloud space: Amazon Web Services (AWS) and Microsoft Azure. While AWS is the largest CSP by a large margin, the adoption of Azure is growing rapidly. But to compare Azure with AWS is like comparing apples and oranges.

Azure is a feature-rich environment that will isolate you from the technical issues and configuration decisions that would otherwise be required to migrate to the cloud. The way Microsoft handles identity management alone will save you multiple decisions and make your users happy as they enjoy SSO and account management features that require more work in other cloud environments.

By way of comparison, AWS is a deep ocean of integrated services with a solution for every need and a price point and performance specification that's hard to match. You are in control, you select and configure the services you want, and AWS handles the rest. Their slogan "we'll handle the infrastructure heavy lifting for you" is pretty accurate.

Each platform has a rich array of services. They can be summarized as follows:

Azure

Virtual Machines (VMs)

Azure lets you dial up the level of service you need. After you select the operating system you want, configuring it for memory-intensive or compute-intensive requirements is easy. The Microsoft offering is geared toward a static model whereby you select the size and number of VMs you want, and you then monitor them and adjust them as necessary, with the billing reflecting your selections. The standard offering includes features such as auto-scaling of servers and load balancing between servers. However, in response to recent pressure on pricing, Microsoft has issued a basic subscription that does not offer these features.

Web Servers

The Azure platform has a comprehensive websites offering. Deploying a website is quite simple, and the main content management systems (CMSs) from Joomla to Drupal are all supported. In addition, the offering includes support for databases such as MySQL and MongoDB.

Storage

Extending your organization's storage requirements into the cloud is facilitated by features such as:

- Tables, whereby any key-value type of data can be stored in massively scalable cloud storage that expands as required
- Blob storage, providing basic disk-based storage for cloud applications
- Files, providing standard Windows file APIs for cloud VMs
- SQL Database provides high-performance relational database operation in the cloud; the service is available on a tiered pricing model.
- Oracle support: while not provided by Microsoft, Oracle database support is available on the Azure platform.

Backup and Recovery

Azure offers a rich backup and restore functionality that is already supported by Windows Server and Microsoft Service Center functions. Using the cloud for backup is a no-brainer since it is secure, inexpensive, and integrated.

Hadoop Services

Azure provides an Apache Hadoop service that allows big data analysis for semi-structured data. Of particular note is the Microsoft Excel interface that allows map-reduce analysis via a de facto standard interface. Moving your big data analysis to the cloud makes a lot of sense since doing so can significantly reduce storage costs and make the data available to a distributed user base.

Application Services

Azure offers a rich environment to support your application development. Message queuing services, API management services, streaming media services, and scheduler and notification services can all be accessed to support your cloud (interfacing to on-premises) applications. Also in the application services category are:

Directory Services

This is a real differentiator for Azure and includes several options to interface with your on-premises Active Directory (AD). Options range from a basic directory synchronization model to a fully federated model that provides SSO between on-premises and cloud-based applications.

Multi-Factor Authentication

The Azure platform was an early adopter of two-factor authentication services. The Microsoft offering is comprehensive, allowing authentication polices to be established for cloud-based applications that mix single-factor with dual-factor requirements. A typical use case: if you are accessing a corporate application from an external location, require a one-time-password login via the user's smartphone. The Windows Device Registration Service is a useful feature in this instance.

Visual Studio Online

Full application development management is facilitated via a cloud-based instance of Visual Studio. This encourages developers to embrace the cloud and, since this is where the future is, the sooner an online version of Visual Studio is established, the better.

BizTalk Services

The application integration engine BizTalk has been around a long time and comes into its own in a cloud environment. The tool allows exchange of information between cloud and on-premises applications and can facilitate the migration-to-cloud task.

SAP Solutions

The Azure environment can now natively host SAP ERP applications to allow SAP customers to offload the compute and database components of running the service. Perhaps the biggest benefit is the ability to manage business partner access to an SAP environment, leveraging features such as two-factor authentication. Global customers will appreciate Azure Network Services support.

Network Services

Azure offers a variety of network services such as Traffic Manager that facilitate load-balancing between Azure data centers and ExpressRoute, which provides a private network connection between data centers for high-performance data-transfer requirements. Specific services include:

Virtual Network

As a way to extend your network into the cloud, Azure provides a way to deploy a virtual private network into the cloud. The facility establishes an encrypted channel between your corporate network and services in Azure to allow you to take advantage of such services as cloud-based backup and cloud-based database services. Big data storage is a candidate for a VPN operation.

Content Delivery Network (CDN)

One of the most innovative aspects of Azure is the ability to manage content that applications, possibly distributed around the globe, require. Partially out of necessity, because Windows applications are quite verbose in regard to network usage, and partially to provide redundancy, application data can be stored with the application. This means that each region in which an application is deployed can hold a local incidence of the data required by the application. This is particularly useful for distributed websites that must render graphical data.

AWS

Just about every facet of information technology is covered by an AWS service offering:

EC2 (Elastic Compute Cloud)

The core offering of AWS is access to raw compute power. With AWS you can "dial up" as few or as many VM cycles as you want. And on top of that, you can configure the service to automatically ratchet up your service as your users demand more. This makes AWS ideal for the testing workload, or for any service profile with a "lumpy" or seasonal load. With the right provisioning tool (and you might need to use a third-party product for this), the service will automatically add more compute power to the mix as demand dictates and remove services as load diminishes, reducing the cost of your subscription.

S3 (Simple Storage Services)

AWS makes it easy to store large amounts of data at very attractive pricing. Users can store any amount of data and allow retrieval from anywhere on the Internet. The service provides secure, scalable storage and supports SOAP and RESTful interfaces.

Amazon RDS

RDS is a service that makes it easy to establish a relational database service in the cloud via a Web service to manage and operate the database. The operator can scale the database operation to meet performance requirements. Operators can select MySQL, Oracle, PostgreSQL, or Aurora database technology.

DynamoDB

If your database requirement is less structured and you want a high-performance storage database, the AWS DynamoDB offering could be just what you require. DynamoDB is AWS's noSQL database. All data is stored in a table, but there is no schema. You don't define columns, and each entry can have any number of attributes

Website Hosting

Adding Web services to your computing mix is a snap with AWS. Simply configure your service with the right DNS and security settings, upload your code, and you're in business. Again AWS will handle the volume, and you can add as many or as few security features as you wish to pay for.

CloudFormation

Managing AWS infrastructure can be daunting, particularly if you need to manage development, test, pre-production, and production environments. CloudFormation provides an interface to make this easier, and will likely result in an overall savings on your AWS bill.

CloudWatch

A very useful feature of the AWS environment is the CloudWatch monitoring service that allows you to keep track of system functions from a remote monitoring station; even a smartphone.

CloudTrail

AWS CloudTrail is a governance tool that logs calls to AWS APIs for tracking purposes. It is useful to know which applications are calling AWS services for account management, billing, and security purposes. The logs are written to a preconfigured S3 storage location.

Redshift

The Redshift service is a data warehouse in the cloud. It uses a basic table structure and an SQL interface. It is competitively priced with a sliding scale depending upon the desired performance.

EMR (Elastic MapReduce)

AWS's big data map reduce offering is called EMR. It is a Hadoop-based service that is ideal for analyzing large data repositories. EMR distributes the workload across multiple EC2 VMs, depending upon the number of nodes configured.

Kinesis

The Kinesis tool provides data-streaming analysis. By pumping your streaming data into Kinesis, you can monitor and analyze it via a graphical display and business intelligence (BI) tools. AWS will automatically configure your storage to meet the requirements of the data stream.

Workspaces (Zocalo)

All CSPs worth their salt provide a document service that allows concurrent modifications to documents. Microsoft Office 365 handles this, as does Google Docs; AWS's answer is a powerful application also known as Zocalo. Not only does it let you collaborate on reports and papers, it also adds IM features and email threads that enhance collaborative activity.

Cloud Deployment

Once the strategy is in place, you must deploy an appropriate solution. While many issues need to be addressed, there are two main concerns.

Risk Management

A risk management approach is highly recommended for any company that seeks to migrate applications to the cloud. The selection of a CSP should include a risk assessment that will guide the process to select an appropriate supplier to provide the required cloud service. While many assessment tools are available, at minimum you should evaluate a service based on three categories of risks[1]:

- Organizational risks such as:
  - o Lock-in to a single provider
  - o Loss of governance over IT services
  - o Cloud service failure
- Technical risks such as:
  - o Malicious insider activity
  - o Management interface compromise
  - o Denial of service (DoS) attack
- Legal risks such as:
  - o Data protection risks
  - o Licensing risks
  - o Changes of jurisdiction risks

Only when the risks are understood can they be managed and disaster be averted.

---

[1] Based on the European Union Agency for Network and Information Security (ENISA) risk management model

A company in the UK moved a customer-facing application to a cloud service. One weekend the database became corrupt, so the IT manager told his staff to call the CSP and ask them to roll back to Friday and then repost transactions from the journal file. Upon calling the CSP, they were advised that they had not purchased the data backup service.

Enterprise Architecture

From a strategy perspective, an organization's enterprise architecture should address cloud services. Organizations that lack an enterprise architecture are paying too much for their IT infrastructure and should expedite the development of at least a technical architecture. This will mandate which operating systems should be supported, and which are deprecated. It should also indicate which type of configurations (patterns) are supported. This will reduce the management cost of the organization's IT infrastructure.

Note: Locating a suitable consultant is not a trivial exercise. It seems many IT architecture consultants tend to make the development of an enterprise architecture overly complex. This is unfortunate because developing an enterprise architecture is not too difficult. There are basically four levels to be addressed by an organization's IT architecture[2]:

- Business systems architecture—how the IT infrastructure will support business unit applications. This includes planning the touchpoints between the applications and the identity management infrastructure. Process maps assist in this understanding.

- Information architecture—indicates the information in the organization's main data stores and how it maps to the requirements of the applications that the organization supports. Entity relationship diagrams are a useful tool.

- Application portfolio—an inventory of the applications used in the organization, which indicates their operating system requirements, storage requirements, and support requirements. This will also include the development plans for each application, so that the enterprise architecture will be used to optimize upgrades—in an application that requires additional identity attributes, the collection and storage of these attributes needs to occur first.

---

[2] Based on the classic MetaGroup (now Gartner) Enterprise Architecture methodology

- Technical architecture—indicates the server infrastructure (and operating system versions), supported technical patterns (e.g., client/server, *n*-tier Web services), supported databases, and guidelines for deployed interfaces. Most organizations will maintain a Web services environment (browser client, Web server, application server, database server); some will have client/server applications, possibly with a standard operating environment deployment model; and some might also support a hub-and-spoke pattern for a mainframe app. The more patterns to support, the more the environment costs to operate and the more complex will be the identity management environment. A Web services environment will typically use a Security Assertion Markup Language (SAML) request to communicate identity attributes, client/server apps will often use LDAP, and a mainframe application will typically require identity attributes to be written to its accounts repository.

Interface Support

A cloud strategy must also address the interfaces to be supported.

As noted in chapter 3, LDAP is not a good solution for cloud apps. This means that today's software developers do not need to learn the intricacies of optimizing LDAP filters; they can work with the Java-based, RESTful API interfaces that they prefer. But these services do represent a potential vulnerability for organizations. There are two basic approaches to the modern identity management task: use a Web service to connect to the data repository, or use an API that supports the programming language of choice to integrate with the IdP service. The latter will generally provide better security and performance; the former requires less programming prowess.

Developer guidelines should be developed and documented to dictate what the various HTTP methods are allowed to do. If an API is developed, both API management and API security controls need to be determined and documented. Engaging a Web developer on the basis of lowest cost is generally unwise.

The protocols shown in Table 5.4 will be a requirement for most cloud-based identity management deployments.

Table 5.4: Required protocols for cloud-based identity management

Protocol	Description
SAML support for requests and assertions	SAML is the prescribed solution for cross-boundary communication of identity data. There are several reasons for this. SAML messages can be digitally signed to ensure they come from approved senders, they can be encrypted without the need for TLS/SSL, and SAML message payloads are typically tagged attributes in XML files, which are ideal for the transmission of user credentials and login tokens.
RESTful API with support for JSON arrays and XML files	HTTP continues to be a popular way to move information around an IP-based network, but HTTP has some shortcomings when it comes to security and performance. Without guidance, programmers are likely to develop interfaces that do not adhere to a security model and provide no management capability. RESTful interfaces are therefore a preferred approach to data interchange. Programmers like such an approach because it means they can use their programming environment of choice, such as Java or C++. Application managers like them because they can expose an API over which they have complete control.
OData native support	OData is a directory interface protocol that is ideally suited to working with modern directories. It is an open protocol that supports modern programming languages and RESTful APIs. With the trend toward NoSQL databases that use a graph database to store data, the OData interface protocol is now widely accepted as the future for both cloud and on-premises environments. This approach to identity storage facilitates the recording of relationship data, which is becoming increasingly important when it comes to identity data management.
OpenID Connect with OAuth token support	OpenID Connect is the protocol of choice for remote, client-based applications that communicate to corporate applications. Apps on smartphones and tablets can securely connect to a service provider (application), and access control can be managed accordingly. A typical deployment will use OAuth to positively identify the device or user of the application.
FIDO	The Fast ID On-line (FIDO) Alliance provides ready-made code that can be used to significantly reduce the time to develop secure and manageable code that facilitates the identification of users connecting from remote locations. There are two main code bases: user-access framework and second-factor experience. Conformance testing services are also available.

Planning a cloud deployment requires defining the protocol support to be put in place so that cloud services comply with organizational security policy.

Conclusion

The cloud provides an ideal opportunity for organizations to rethink their IdM environment and plan an approach that will not only allow them to manage their cloud-based future but also exploit the capabilities of the cloud to drive an innovative and agile organization.

Possibly the biggest issue when considering cloud migration is the changes it makes to the way IT is managed within an organization. In some companies, cloud is seen as outside IT's purview because the cloud gives business managers the laxity to "do their own thing" without the constraints imposed by the IT department, which has developed processes that not only take time but have a tangible cost to the company. This is dangerous since it removes cloud infrastructure from the controls that are required to ensure good governance. While the board of directors might not realize it, cloud represents a potential "wild frontier" of computing that can lead to significant trouble in the absence of governance.

So how can an IT operation assimilate the cloud without destroying its attractive qualities: agile, inexpensive, and powerful?

Establishment of a multi-functional team, with IT department involvement, to handle requests for cloud infrastructure should be considered. This team would ensure that appropriate architecture alignment is observed, the appropriate reviews occur, and the right vendor partners are engaged. Then IT can disengage and leave the CSP to configure servers, establish databases, and manage service requests.

One thing is for sure: cloud is such an imperative that there is no "do nothing" option, and deploying an identity solution for cloud services is a business imperative.

Use Case: University

Scenario	Uni is a medium-sized university with 40,000 students and 8,000 staff. There are five faculties across three campuses. The HR system is a commercial product that runs on-premises on a Windows infrastructure. The student admin system is an open source Linux product installed on-premises. The service desk system is a corporate system that runs on a public cloud service; an extract from the University's AD service is sent to the service desk application each night. There are eight large SaaS apps being used in the Uni, including the learning management system (LMS), with varying amounts of nightly synchronization of identity data.

Strategy	Uni has identified the synchronization of identity data to the cloud as a risk that requires mitigation. Reducing the number of data stores and improving the security of the identity stores is desired. Since there are no plans to move the HR and student admin system in the near term, it will be necessary to maintain the on-premises AD infrastructure in the short term.
Solution	The development of a cloud migration strategy is recommended to avoid proliferation of identity stores in the cloud. This should include the establishment of a cloud-based identity provider service to support the current and planned SaaS applications. This could be the data store currently supporting the service desk system if it supports SAML. In this instance, the need is to ensure that the current attributes synchronized to the service contain the attributes required by the other relying applications. In the medium term, plans to locate the student admin system on cloud services should be developed. Considerations include the selection of private versus public cloud—this should occur using a risk management approach. The availability of auto-scaling on most cloud services would be a significant advantage during enrollment times in order to accommodate the increased load. Migration of the HR system to cloud services will likely be a longer-term consideration since it will have more touchpoints with on-premises systems. This means that, for a time, it will be necessary to operate with staff identities provisioned on-premises and student identities provisioned in the cloud. This is unlikely to be a major concern since staff and students are typically in separate email domains, simplifying the determination of the appropriate IdP to be used to authenticate users. If an authenticating user is a staff member, the on-premises AD will be used. If a student is authenticating, the cloud-based IdP service would be used. For staff who require access to the LMS, a federated approach will maintain SSO. In the long term, the HR system will be migrated to cloud services, and a single repository should be deployed that supports the protocols required by the relying applications. This will include the SAML standard. It will also require support for API access to the IdP, so that higher levels of authentication can be supported. An OData interface will likely be a requirement. The SCIM standard will likely be required for provisioning.

Q & A

Q. For a startup business, should an on-premises data center be a consideration, or would cloud services be adopted from the start?

A. It is hard to imagine any circumstances in which an on-premises environment should be considered for a startup. The advantages that cloud offers suggest it unlikely that any on-premises infrastructure would make operational or economic sense. Being able to avoid the need to hire system admins and network specialists and being able to rely on a CSP for systems upgrades, data storage, and services such as auto-scaling and security services are compelling arguments for the adoptions of cloud services.

The only issues that might suggest on-premises infrastructure are regulatory controls such as data sovereignty restrictions on out-of-jurisdiction storage of personnel data or network latency requirements that might preclude the use of cloud infrastructure. To address these cases, most CSPs can provide appropriate services to accommodate such requirements, and most CSPs can recommend communication services companies to provide the appropriate network performance.

Q. Given that savings on system administrative personnel is a major justification for migration to the cloud, what if there are impediments to reducing IT staff?

A. Although there are other economic justification for migrating to the cloud, a reduction in system administrative staff is a major incentive for moving applications to cloud-based services. The time period during which on-premises and cloud services are maintained should ideally be minimized, and the timeframe during which redundant services are maintained should be factored into the migration planning. Note: Some corporate staff will be needed to manage CSP services or support infrastructure, such as a key management service if a customer-provided keys approach is required.

Companies adopting an IaaS approach in which they must maintain their own systems in the cloud will need to maintain some system administration staff.

Q. Network services suppliers providing IaaS are increasingly offering sophisticated networking capabilities. To what degree should these be factored into a cloud migration strategy?

A. Software-defined networking (SDN) is moving ahead at an accelerating rate. SDN has the capability to offer customers sophisticated networking services that support IaaS offerings and identity-based access control of network functions.

SDN services should be considered in the development of a cloud strategy and will be most beneficial for enterprises operating in a global environment that requires different access to services in different geographies. The future is one in which SDN services leverage an organization's identity provider service for access control to network services.

Chapter 6

BYOD: Why It's Good for You

I still remember when I first saw a car with seatbelts. I thought it was a stupid idea that restricted your freedom to move around the vehicle—sliding across the bench seat or climbing into the back seat for a change whenever you wanted. Now the bench seat is gone, and cars are too small to climb into the back. But now I don't feel comfortable without a seatbelt, either. It's a similar situation with mobile devices. When smartphones first came on the scene, many network administrators could not conceive of allowing them on the network. But things have moved on since then, and connecting to the corporate network via a phone or tablet (or a "phablet"—a generic term for a phone or tablet) is commonplace. In fact, in many ways there are better controls available for phablets than there are for corporate devices directly connected to the company network. It is now possible to positively identify anyone via a smartphone to a high level of assurance.

There are two sides to the BYOD coin: users and corporate. For the user, the tablet has become an indispensable item. Millennials don't know what to do with a 12-inch screen; anything larger than 4.5 inches is considered superfluous. Of course, it's the mobile factor that makes it so attractive. Being able to carry your terminal around in your pocket is most advantageous. But it has its downsides: it's not easy to get a smartphone in the front pocket of your jeans, so smartphones are often carried in a rear pocket and are thus at risk of loss or damage. Anecdotal evidence suggests that at any point in time 10 percent of young people are using a device with a broken screen. But the older generation, too, are becoming wedded to their smartphones, and older people are increasingly adopting tablet technology. If your target market is "gray-haired nomads," you ignore phablets at your peril. So having a responsive website to support phablets is now a necessity.

Given the ubiquity of phablets, from a corporate perspective it makes sense to accommodate these devices in the organization's IT strategy. If users are willing to provide their own devices, this means the company does not need to go to the time and cost of supplying them. The first decision to be made is device ownership: should the company issue staff corporate smartphones so that they can exert control over what's on the device, or should they get the user to download an app that creates a partition on the device that can be wiped in the event that the owner leaves the company's employ? If the latter, should the company reimburse staff who elect to use their own smartphones?

Phablets Are King

When it comes to smartphones, there are two areas in which companies must develop a strategy:

Consumer

The rise of the consumer in the second half of the last century came about largely because of competition that arose in local marketplaces. It was important that companies knew their customers, so that they could give them good service and keep them coming back to purchase. But then, as business progressed, supermarkets replaced local stores, manufacturing moved offshore, and products became commodities. The consumer became a commodity, too—merely a unit responsible for a small percentage of a market share number.

But that all changed with smartphones, apps, and big data.

Suddenly companies were interested in our thoughts about their products, our purchasing patterns, and our propensity to purchase. As consumers, we are entering into a brave new world in which companies will know how to interest us in their products or services. They will know when we are likely to purchase, and they will have the ability to contact us when that time comes.

Gone are the days when we valued our privacy; now we just want convenience. We don't want to carry loyalty cards, discount coupons, or even credit cards. Because we will always have our phone with us, the smartphone is the ideal tool to leverage for promotional purposes.

Retailers are responding with support for near field communication (NFC) devices, so that we can make our payments directly from our phones. They use beacon transmitters to beam special promotions to us, and they offer Wi-Fi services so that they know when we're in their store. The smartphone has won.

Enterprise

But that's not all, folks. We also take our phones to work, where we sit down in front of our PCs and login to the network to perform our job duties. Then we get up from our desk to go to a meeting or go for a lunch break, and we take our phones with us. Even though we have a powerful computing device with network connectivity in our pockets or handbags, we can no longer be contacted and can't respond to requests. While older folk might find this advantageous, to younger people it is incongruous.

From the company's viewpoint, the smartphone represents an opportunity with potentially substantial benefit:

- Staff provide their own devices.
- Staff can be contacted more readily and can respond more quickly.
- The company can support a better work-life balance by reducing "desk-present" time.

The response by industry has been fragmented. Some businesses still actively dissuade staff from using their phones on corporate premises, whereas others have readily accepted smartphones and exploit them for business purposes.

But there are potential problems:

- When a staff member accesses a corporate application from their smartphone, how do you know it's them?
- If staff access corporate data from their own devices, how can you be sure the data is not made visible to people who should not have it?
- If a staff member leaves the organization, how can you be sure corporate data is removed from their phones?

Identities and Entities

Our identity management task now needs to expand to encompass entity management. Both retailers and enterprises alike have similar issues: is the user who is making a purchase the person they purport to be? Is the device accessing corporate systems adequately protected? There are varying degrees of assurance in the answer to these questions. If a smartphone user is buying groceries, the level of assurance is quite low. At worst, if the user is buying goods on behalf of someone else, it might skew the marketing data, which is of little consequence. But if the user is placing an order on a company's production system, there is a requirement for a higher level of assurance and potentially a need for non-repudiation.

Similarly, if a user's device is jailbroken but they are just browsing the company's website, it is of little consequence. But if they are using a corporate app to access the company's data repository containing restricted documents, it could be very important.

For any system that allows access from the Internet, it is important to understand the required level of assurance, and to design a system that provides the required level of authentication and accountability. In designing a system to meet our company's requirements, there are multiple options available to us, which we'll now explore.

Business Imperative

Although the use of smartphones is an accepted practice, and most organizations have developed policies and procedures to accommodate their use in accessing corporate facilities, BYOD remains a contentious issue in some circles. IT staff want to restrict smartphone access or functionality, and users resent this as unnecessary and retrograde. Both are reasonable responses to this potentially emotive issue.

IT organizations often fear loss of control rather than potential security breaches. So while the stated cause for imposition of constraints might be one issue, the real reason might be slightly different. It is important to identify the real objections and deal with them. For instance, if the real issue is a "loss of control" by the IT department, from a corporate perspective, finding a way to cede governance to IT staff might be best.

In regard to security concerns, there are many ways to avoid potential security breaches via mobile devices, by enabling any of multiple protection methods.

It is important that a balance is reached, as Figure 6.1 shows. This balance is between the obvious benefits of smartphones—access from anywhere at any time, and the dangers associated with such access—the security risks of having corporate data on external devices and the requirement to manage regulatory issues such as data protection legislation.

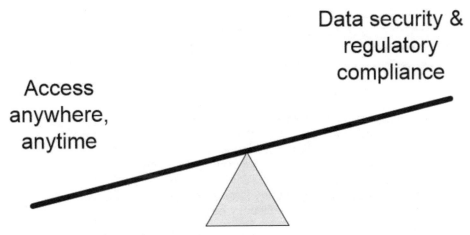

Figure 6.1: Balancing access versus security in BYOD

Security issues can be overcome via restrictions on the type and quantity of data that can be sent to a smartphone, using data-loss protection technology that inhibits the exfiltration of protected documents for the corporate network, or by deploying a mobile device management (MDM) environment that manages smartphones by creating a protected area on the phone that is managed by the company, not the user.

Compliance issues can also be controlled by an MDM approach (see the MDM section on page 118), or a native app that's developed for all corporate business, with controls placed on controlled information such as personally identifiable information (PII) or credit card numbers to ensure adherence to both the spirit and letter of applicable legislation.

The bottom line is to define policy and deploy technology that allows staff to use a device of their choosing to access applications and services, so that productivity is maximized while corporate guidelines are observed.

In the corporate world, tablets might be treated differently from smartphones. Two characteristics of tablets make them particularly useful devices for corporate deployment:

- Touch-screen enables control functions to be displayed and actuated by just touching the screen. This also makes tablets ideal for capturing survey results or marking test results. It makes little sense, for example, for a driving test inspector to capture test results on paper forms, which must be transcribed into the test record system.

- Mobility means that a tablet is an ideal tool for any job that is not tied to a desk. This is particularly attractive for any job that requires constant monitoring during lunch breaks or on-call situations in which staff must be constantly contactable.

> An innovative use of phablets was identified at a utility company that uses them for displaying status and providing control of the hydro-electricity generators. From the handheld device, it is possible to monitor spot prices of electricity and bring generators online quickly. Since prices are higher in the evening, this use of phablets allowed the company to extend their monitoring and control operations significantly beyond normal business hours.

IT staff should actively evaluate corporate situations in which business applications can significantly benefit from phablet technology.

There are basically three factors to be considered: how are devices to be managed, how are applications going to be managed, and how is information to be protected?

Managing Devices

An organization has multiple technology decisions to make in regard to managing external devices. Managing an external device requires users to allow a level of control over their device, as shown in Table 6.1.

Table 6.1: Technology considerations for managing external devices

Technology	Description
Data encryption	Ensure device settings encrypt data being stored on the device. This requires users to enable account protection using features such as a password, screen swipe, or hand gesture in order to log in and be able to see the data. Increasingly, the use of passwords is declining in favor of the use of device capabilities for login, which is preferable to entering data into a small screen.
Device management	Disabling device facilities can improve security. If capabilities such as the device camera, network connectivity, and access to contacts are not required, they should be disabled when the corporate profile is in use.
Establish corporate controls	Such controls include remote locking and device wiping for staff who leave the company or lose their device. Some tools enable automatic wiping of the corporate area in the event of extended periods of inactivity.

Managing Applications

Enterprises must determine policies to govern smartphone users' access to corporate data. Some companies choose to only allow access via a Web browser. Such a policy enables server-side control to be maintained and places restrictions on data exfiltration. This also has the benefit of enabling the same Web server to be used for application access by on-premises PCs and external devices. Such websites must be responsive—that is, accommodating the smaller screen size of mobile devices.

Another option is to only allow corporate data to be accessed via a corporate app. Table 6.2 shows several data-access options.

Table 6.2: Data-access options for corporate smartphone use

Option	Description
Operating system support	The support for operating systems (iOS, Android, Windows, or BlackBerry) should be made based on user preference and security policy. Given that the app is corporately developed, there are no issues regarding virus concerns.
Protocol support	The de facto standard is OpenID Connect. Options include the use of OAuth tokens or stored certificates issued at the time of download that can positively identify a device.
Biometrics	Smartphone capabilities such as swipe, gestures, or voice-print can be used to positively identify users.
FIDO	The use of FIDO devices as part of the app initiation or even use of a fingerprint or other biometric facility can ensure that the login is interactive (i.e., not a machine login).

The use of an app allows other security options to be deployed. Apps can be "wrapped" in a communications mechanism that ensures the confidentiality, integrity, and availability of the service. This can be achieved by using any of a number of methods, such as a dedicated API or software containerization.

Managing Information

Secure information sharing in the mobile environment is not easy. Most phone usage occurs in public areas, all phones come with insecure facilities that users want to use, and some users fail to implement any access security on their phones. Organizations are faced with decisions regarding how to leverage the smartphone platform but at the same time enable secure information sharing. Table 6.3 lists some considerations for enabling secure information sharing by corporate smartphone users.

Table 6.3: Information-sharing options for corporate smartphone use

Option	Description
Phone screen visible in public places	There is no way to know who might be looking over the shoulder of an employee while he or she is using a smartphone in a public area. A typical response is to use exfiltration controls, so that sensitive corporate data is not exported to mobile devices. This can be achieved via a data sharing technology that restricts smartphone clients from opening attachments, or by redirecting documentation available on remote devices. Another option is to use the mobile device's GPS capabilities to geo-fence it or restrict access during non-business hours.

Login services	Because some phone users do not use any form of login protection, it is important to implement a policy that ensures that not everyone who turns on a phone can access corporate applications' sensitive data that might be available to a mobile device. Virtually all corporate applications that are available via a phone or tablet require users to implement some form of access control. Username and password is not the best login method for the mobile device because of the limitations of the user interface. Today's devices support a better user experience via the use of screen swipes or gestures, which provide a secure alternative to password authentication.
Secure information sharing	Technology exists to include smartphones and tablets in an organization's secure information sharing environment. This will usually require the user to download a client that secures data in transit and data in use on the device. Corporate data is not available during public use of the device. These clients typically invoke rights management technology that determines the access rights a user is granted to individual documents (e.g., read only, edit, print, save).

Device Type

Android

The Android operating system is currently most widely used because of the number of suppliers that have adopted the OS for their mobile devices. It is, however, considered the "wild west" of mobile device operating systems because of the largely unregulated nature of the application development environment. It is easy to develop an Android app and deploy it via the Google Play store. It will quickly get reviewed and assessed in the stringent court of public opinion.

iOS

In contrast, the Apple iOS environment is strictly controlled by Apple. Anyone who wants to deploy an iOS must pay to do so. Apps are reviewed, and a level of conformance to standards is imposed. This means that there is much less malware in the iOS environment and greater governance over the system facilities that an app can access. This has led some organizations to support only iOS devices because they are considered more secure. As we shall see, this is a fallacious argument. Corporations can exert appropriate controls over the Android environment, if this is a requirement.

Windows

Microsoft Windows is on its ascendancy as a tablet and smartphone operating system. The market success of the Surface tablet and the ubiquity of the Windows 10 operating system across multiple devices types mean that Windows-based phones are increasingly attractive to those who want interoperability across their PCs, tablets, and smartphones. Although iOS and Android devices can run the popular Office applications, those applications' functionality is restricted. For full interoperability, it is necessary to be running the Windows operating system.

BlackBerry

Although BlackBerry was the first to deploy a widely available secure environment for smartphones, the BlackBerry phone is now in its decline. There are too few popular apps available for the BlackBerry device, and although BlackBerry Limited has two innovative devices, users—particularly millennials—want to access to the latest apps, and these are typically not available on the BlackBerry.

Managing Mobiles

Organizations that want to support mobile devices often deploy a solution to manage their mobile device "fleet" and assume that this is the right response to protecting themselves from the nefarious behavior, intentional or otherwise, that is often associated with mobile device usage. There are two things wrong with this approach. First, often it does not adequately accommodate user requirements. Second, often it fails to consider that the mobile device environment is part of the wider corporate environment, and that ensuring access to corporate applications from mobile devices must be both enabled and adequately managed.

MDM

MDM tools provide several useful features: corporate applications can be restricted to operate in controlled memory, and managed storage lets the company restrict access to corporate data in situations such as the geolocation of the device. The corporate memory can also be wiped in the event that the user leaves the company's employ or if the device is not accessed in a set number of days, indicating the phone may have been lost.

An MDM product will provide good endpoint management of mobile devices that enable application and data controls. Users will be required to adopt corporate control of their device, or a device provided by the company, and will go through a registration process to enroll the device in the corporate MDM environment.

An MDM solution will also instill a security consciousness within an organization because it will force users to set up login security on their phone and will identify devices that have been jailbroken; behind the scenes it will encrypt the phone's backup. MDM will also enable better governance to be established with logging and reporting functionality for KPI measurements and compliance checks. An MDM solution also reduces the impact of mobile device management on IT resources. For supported devices, it becomes easier for users to "do it all themselves"; for non-supported devices, no time is wasted trying to make things work. As new devices come on the market, IT can modify the MDM solution to accommodate the features of the new device, and as users migrate to new phones, they will enjoy the benefits of support for new features.

Another benefit of an MDM for an enterprise is the deployment capability that it provides. Device enrollment will often be incorporated with the establishment of a standard operating environment (SOE) for mobile devices that will install VPN software and other features that an enterprise might require; but this is getting closer to an EMM solution, discussed in the next section.

> An Asian airline deployed an MDM solution to allow staff access to email from their cell phones and to access corporate documents. The system was not well documented; most users failed to correctly prepare their phone, complete the download, and configure the client.
>
> While IT resources were not adversely affected, each deployment regularly disrupted others in the workgroup who became involved in assisting their peers. Better testing and documentation would have saved the organization significant cost.

EMM

Enterprise Mobility Management (EMM) goes further. The whole concept of EMM is that the device is not just an endpoint for access to specific data, it's an integral part of the corporate IT environment and must be enrolled in all aspects of the functionality provided by the technology, and the governance exerted over it. This means that the device must be enabled with the same controls and be subjected to the same deployment management as any other device. Thus a mobile SOE will be deployed for mobile devices that will ensure appropriate authentication facilities, including multi-factor authentication and device monitoring, with operating system and jailbreak status checks.

With EMM, a mobile device is a lot more useful. Applications written for mobile clients can be monitored and debugged. Transactions undertaken on mobiles can be subjected to the same vigilance as those conducted from other devices; in fact, there are more options to support non-repudiable transactions from mobile devices than from a standard PC.

It is important, then, before simply deploying an MDM, for organizations to consider the breadth of their requirements and ensure that the selected vendor can accommodate the level of mobile device management that the organization requires.

To BYOD, or Not to BYOD?

The term *BYOD* has come to mean any mobile device access to corporate services. This is, of course, not the case. We now come to the thorny issue of whether or not to allow users to attach their own devices to the corporate network. Some companies dissuade their users from using their personal devices and have a policy that states that BYOD is not supported. But many of these companies are not vigilant, because being vigilant is expensive, and so they "look the other way" even though they know what is happening. This is poor practice. It means that organizations are condoning prohibited behavior.

Then there are those organizations in which users are left to their own devices to access corporate resources from device browsers and to access corporate email from the mail programs provided on their devices.

At the other end of the spectrum are those organizations that do not allow any access from mobile devices. Such organizations may prohibit mobile-device use on company premises and require mobile phones to be "checked" and stored in lockers when employees enter their facilities.

A middle ground between these extremes is probably appropriate for most organizations. Staff should be allowed to use their phones—it's part of a healthy work-life balance, but controls should be implemented and enforced. This means that companies need to deploy some form of MDM/EMM solution, which means a decision is required regarding personally owned devices. Companies must decide where on the continuum depicted in Figure 6.2 their device ownership policies lie.

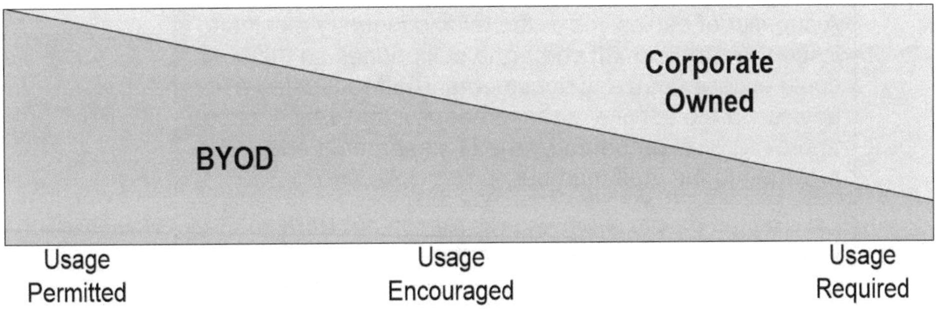

Figure 6.2: Device ownership continuum

At the left side of the continuum, use of smartphones is totally at the users' discretion. Staff use their phone's mail apps to access email, and the phone's browser to access Web apps to which they have entitlements. It isn't particularly easy to use these apps; users will have to enter passwords, and the apps may not be optimized for mobile devices. In these circumstances, the company does get some advantages with staff being more accessible, often working after hours. But there is not a sufficient benefit to motivate the company to reimburse a staff member for using their phone for corporate business and assist in paying phone plan charges. Staff members' recompense comes in the form of better work-life balance.

In the middle, use of mobile devices is encouraged. The company recognizes the benefits of allowing such access and actively encourages it. Here, companies will want to exert some influence over device configuration, and potentially selection; for example, some organizations mandate that only iOS devices can be used for corporate access. Under these circumstances, it is likely that companies should consider reimbursement of staff for device purchase and potential subsidy of staff phone plans.

Companies might require smartphone use as part of a staff member's job requirements. If staff are required to move between venues regularly, and still be available for online meetings, a mobile device is the obvious solution. In such cases, organizations should consider providing corporate devices for users. The devices then become part of company-issued assets that are used in the course of employees in performing their job responsibilities. If companies issue their staff smartphones, they can then exert much more influence over the device configuration and enable greater functionality. Corporate applications can be loaded on a company device that will allow users to control processes and respond to alerts and alarms in a fully managed environment.

A supplier of explosives to the mining industry elected to issue their senior staff corporate cell phones so they could access company documents. Staff requested a device via the service management system which, once approved, was prepared by the IT department and provided to the staff member.

On exit, the de-provisioning process did not work so well. While many staff did return their phones, the company failed to recoup 30 percent of issued devices.

Mobile Strategy

The widespread adoption of MDM solutions suggests that some companies are spending more than they need to, these solutions are not inexpensive, or they have been lulled into a false sense of security assuming they are adequately protected when in fact their staff have been given inappropriate access to sensitive corporate systems. A better approach is to develop a mobile strategy that is targeted at the organization's real requirement. Although developing such a strategy is not difficult, it is more time consuming. It is a worthwhile investment of time that can save a lot of money by avoiding either the deployment of an expensive solution when it isn't needed, or an inadequate system that results in data loss. It will be much better if this analysis occurs before it has to.

Policy

The most important point to get right is the setting of policy. At the very least, a simple policy should be documented and made readily available to staff and even business partners that use their mobile devices to access corporate applications. The policy should cover items such as restrictions on the storage of corporate information on personal devices, agreement to company audit of personal devices, and the user's right to compensation for the use of personally supplied devices.

The Protocols

OpenID Connect

OpenID Connect is a widely used technology for user authentication in cloud environments. It started life as OpenID and underwent a major release to provide more extensive functionality that has made it the technology of choice for large user populations. OpenID Connect is the protocol of choice to leverage pubic identity provider services such as Facebook, GoogleID, and LinkedIn to authenticate users to low-assurance applications. This means that users can use one of their social networking logins to access corporate services. This has obvious benefits when users are working from small screens that make it difficult to keep entering usernames and passwords. It also, arguably, improves security because users will not need to "write down" their login credentials in places where they might be found.

It would be misleading to leave OpenID Connect in the social networking space. The level of assurance is defined by the identity provider services being accessed and must be matched to the level of assurance required by the service being accessed. If OpenID Connect is integrated to a high-assurance service, the technology can meet enterprise-level requirements. It can utilize OAuth tokens issued by corporate servers to authenticate staff to a high level.

Having said that, OpenID Connect is the technology of choice when federating social logins.

OAuth

A related technology is OAuth. OAuth originated from software developers who needed a lightweight method of access control that was appropriate for mobile phones and social login environments. The protocol is most widespread in the mobile device space and is the protocol of choice for native apps to use for authenticating users to services. OAuth tokens are small, unlike SAML, and an OAuth payload will typically use JSON to pass data attributes—which is preferred by programmers.

There are two configuration models for OAuth: two-legged authentication, whereby the users/device token validates the access from the mobile device, and a three-legged approach, in which the user's token must be validated by an authentication server before access is granted. The former can be used by a native app where a token associated with a user, or a device, is used as part of an enrollment activity, or an application can embed a token that authenticates the user as part of a logon activity. The three-legged approach requires an authentication server to approve a user's authority to access controlled resources. It can be managed in real time and provides a higher level of assurance. It also can be used to maintain sessions and has a concept of a "refresh" token for approving session-timeout extensions.

OAuth is ideal for APIs whereby a user's access credentials can be checked before passing them to the requested resource. That is, the developer can control the authentication process commensurate with the assurance level of the protected resources behind the API. In this instance, the API management and security functionality provide the governance over user access policy.

SAML vs. OAuth

SAML is used mostly in the authentication of a user to a Web application. The user's browser accommodates the login process of redirecting between the requested resource and the identity provider, and it supports single sign-on (SSO). SAML payloads are typically heavyweight, with XML and long token lengths. SAML is ideal for enterprise deployments, particularly those that have an enterprise architecture that define information requirements in the organization and a taxonomy for data elements used within business applications and processes. SAML is best suited to an environment where fast processors and good communication links are available.

OAuth (three-legged) is a more cut-down protocol with minimalist payloads and short token lengths. This makes it ideal for mobile devices and 3G communication links. OAuth is typically used for single-app authentication. Since most public IdPs support OAuth, this makes it the protocol of choice for mobile device access to back-end systems. Table 6.4 compares SAML and OAuth.

Table 6.4: SAML-OAuth summary comparison

	SAML	OAuth
Environment	Enterprise—cross-boundary authentication	Consumer-based, authorization to APIs
Typical client	Web browser	Native apps and cell phone browser
Application	User to enterprise or SaaS apps	Consumer to SaaS apps
Payload	Large, typically XML-based	Small JSON arrays
Security	Rich, digitally signed with many security options	Random tokens—quick to validate, fewer options

FIDO

An even higher level of assurance can be provided via Fast IDentity Online (FIDO) Alliance technology. While initially positioned as password-replacement technology, FIDO can go far beyond that. There are multiple solutions offered by members of the alliance, but they all adhere to the FIDO specification. Some solutions are hardware-related requiring, for instance, a USB device to be plugged in to the user's system in order to log on to a protected resource, or there are software solutions with FIDO-compliant code embedded in applications. The hardware device solutions can allow innovative solutions such as user-present functionality, which requires the user to physically touch the device in order to log in.

FIDO has been adopted by some handset manufacturers and is built into their software stack. PayPal and Google are two major proponents of FIDO.

Device Registration

It must be mentioned that there are other options for elevating the assurance level of access from mobile devices. Device registration immediately raises a user's level of authentication because it adds a validated second factor.

Microsoft offers a device registration service whereby only devices that have been approved can access protected resources. This can cover both on-premises applications and cloud applications. In the cloud, there are additional authentication events that can be utilized during the authentication process. Both Microsoft Azure and Amazon Web Services support two-factor authentication. When invoked, the authentication process will send a message to, or ring, the phone of the user and provide a PIN code that must be entered into the user's device to complete the login process. Some authentication mechanisms use a swipe or gesture to positively identify a user. The use of multiple factors during the login process significantly heightens the authentication assurance level of the access[1].

The Future of Device Support

It's no secret that, by a long margin, more development is happening in the smartphone space than for any other device type. This means that we need to develop strategies to adopt mobile devices as part of our IT environment.

It is unlikely they will stay in their current format. With flexible screens and wearable devices under intense development, the bits we get to interface with—screens and microphones—will evolve dramatically over the coming years.

---

[1] Adopting a second factor is a better mechanism for increasing the level of authentication than strengthening a single-factor mechanism (i.e. forcing long passwords).

Communication capabilities will also develop dramatically. 5G is optimized for data, and our phones will respond accordingly. A major area of development is in augmented reality; our phone will know more about where we are than we do. The phone will share some of this information with us: as we enter the shopping mall, the coffee shop with a 2-for-1 offer will beep us, the bank will be alerted that we have arrived for our meeting, and our car will let us know when our three-hour free parking is expiring.

In the corporate environment, we'll use our phone's NFC capabilities to enter restricted areas, multisite virtual meetings will be normal, and our devices will increasingly be used as control devices for the lights, room temperature, and presence indicators. Rooms will "switch on" when we enter them and "switch off" into a dormant state when we leave. Entering the dormant state will switch off the data projector, turn down the lights, close the window blinds, and turn down the heat or air conditioning.

Voice recognition will also become the norm. No longer will users activate applications via the screen, and they definitely won't be keying in passwords. Applications will respond to voice commands, and voice input will be used to record meetings—not audio but text. This also impinges on identity management. It is now easy to authenticate a person by a voice print, and two-factor authentication using voice recognition is becoming commonplace.

Holographic capabilities are also developing fast. Being able to see 3D images will significantly improve the usefulness of a smartphone for inspection of an item of interest, or for remote medicine, where a specialist advises remotely located attendees on a medical procedure.

Conclusion

There is no doubt that smartphone technology is here to stay. Organizations must decide on the device support they want to leverage, to what degree they want to support BYOD, and the control environment (e.g., MDM, EMM) they want to adopt for phablets.

Failure to make these decisions severely hampers an organization's agility and ability to take advantage of innovative work practices. Just as seatbelts are part of life, so smartphones are a reality we cannot, and should not, ignore.

Use Case: Regional Hospital

Scenario	Medicali General Hospital is a community medical facility in a city with a population of 500,000 people. There are three operating theatres and, during business hours, a medical photographer is on staff. After hours, operating theatre staff use their smartphones when they need to record a condition or document a procedure. The resultant security issues and patient consent concerns have led to a review of the practice of medical staff's use of their personal smartphone cameras.
Strategy	The enterprise architecture for the hospital was amended to include smartphones. It was determined to support Android and iOS in the first instance. The entity relationship diagrams were updated to indicate the data sets to be supported for operating theatre use of smartphones.
Solution	A smartphone app was developed for operating theatre personnel to download to their phones to securely record photos, video, and audio content against a patient's procedure. The app automatically identifies the theatre in which the procedure is occurring and checks the theatre schedule to identify the patient. As the content is submitted, it is written to the record of the procedure and linked to the patient's record. The ease of use of the app and reduction in the effort otherwise required to link a photo to a procedure make it the preferred option for recording operating theatre procedure events. This significantly reduced the incidence of non-authorized devices being used to record medical events.

Q & A

Q. How should an organization that is considering the use of smartphones as input devices select the most appropriate authentication mechanism?

A. Excluding military applications, it is recommended that a company keep its strategy simple, possibly adopting a three-level approach:

Low	Mobile devices can access corporate email and calendaring systems with username and password established at the time of configuration. No access to corporate information is required, and no application or device intervention is required.
Medium	Mobile devices are used to access corporate systems and to capture data to be written to corporate applications. A corporate app is required to be downloaded from the company's website, and a certificate is placed on the phone to identify the user. The app resides in protected memory, which can be remotely wiped by the company in the event of compromise or when the user leaves the company. There is no compensation for those that choose to use the app.
High	Mobile phones are used to access documents for team members who are working on a sensitive development project. The app uses a certificate for identifying the smartphone. It uses a FIDO device with fingerprint capture, and the app accesses the phone's geo-positioning feature. The FIDO devices are provided free of charge, and users are financially compensated for using the app.

Q. What are the pros and cons of using a mobile device management (MDM) solution?

A. An MDM solution such as AirWatch or MobileIron provides a way to establish a "corporate" solution on mobile devices that is under the control of the enterprise. This enables some facilities to be put in place that let the enterprise manage the distribution of corporate data to the mobile device and delete data when the owner leaves the company's employ or the device is lost. MDM also enables the company to establish rules such as geographic limitations on opening the corporate area of the smartphone. If the device is outside the prescribed area, corporate documents would not be accessible.

However, the selection of an MDM solution ought to go beyond simply enabling applications that should be accessible on mobile devices. The solution should consider items such as:

- Device support—is there a particular device type (e.g., touchscreen tablet) to be supported?

- Corporate system access—what is the requirement for devices to access corporate applications? Is there a need to manage access to specific applications and to integrate with corporate access control or intrusion detection systems?

- Is there a necessity for cross-device development—for example, testing and debugging support?

If extended functionality is required, a more enterprise-oriented solution that integrates with the company's enterprise IT infrastructure, such as CA Technologies' MDM or IBM MaaS360 EMM, might be more appropriate.

Q. Should companies reimburse users for using their personal smartphones for company business?

A. There is no right or wrong choice here. Typically, users should be given the opportunity to use their own devices without reimbursement, but should also be given the opportunity to have a corporate device if their job requires it. Most users will want mobile device access to corporate mail and the business appointment calendar but not the inconvenience of carrying two devices. These staff will elect to adopt the BYOD solution. Some users will want to keep business and private activities completely separate and will apply for a corporate device.

The main reason to consider reimbursing users for the use of their own devices would be because of an employment agreement that mandates it.

Chapter 7

Internet of Things: You Can't Avoid the Inevitable

The Internet of Things (IoT) is upon us. "What does that mean?" you may ask. Well, it means you had better get ready to use your identity management environment to support access to "things." "But we don't do that," you reply. "Why not?" is my response. It is highly likely that there are business processes within your organization that could benefit from the deployment of things. So when you finally get pulled into the 21st century, you will need to plan for more than just people accessing your systems.

Over the past few years, we have experienced a dramatic reduction in the cost of devices that monitor things and actuators that control things. It is now very inexpensive to remotely measure things and to turn things on and off. It's important that companies evaluate the potential of exploiting these cost reductions and take advantage of the opportunity that they afford.

But before you invest in IoT, there are a few questions you will need to answer, as shown in Table 7.1

Table 7.1: Questions to ask when assessing IoT

Collection Devices	Control Devices
How will you associate ownership with collected data?	Who should be able to access control devices?
How will you protect data, and how will you give owners access to it?	What level of access should approved users be given?
How will you allow users to share data with authorized persons?	Should users be able to delegate access to others?

If you can answer these questions (see the section "So, What Can Be Done?" on page 137), improvements to numerous business applications await.

Devices as Things

So the next question is: "What's a 'thing,' and what does it want?"

Things can basically be divided into two categories: those that can measure something (*sensors*) and those that control something (*actuators*). Sensors can be as simple as a thermometer that measures the temperature inside a house, or as complex as the monitor that measures a car's fuel mixture as the vehicle accelerates.

In a manufacturing environment, IoT data can be very valuable. IoT data can, for example, show how much product is being produced and the rate of rejects, how many people are on a ship's bridge and their ranks, or the current rate of inventory depletion, and project when the manufacturing department will run out of raw material. Increasingly we need to share this data with others in the company or business partners outside the company. How do we control the release of sensitive information, and how do we restrict its usage to approved persons?

Actuators are even more interesting. They can either be discreet, turning something on or off, or they can be a continuous process-control device such as a valve moderating the flow of a gas, liquid, or granular solids in accordance with external stimuli. Adding cement, aggregate, and water into a cement mixer is an example. It should be obvious that restricting access to actuators to authorized personnel is very important.

The Impact on Our Lives

It's hard to underestimate the impact that IoT technology will have on our lives. While the last generation saw immense changes in terms of television, audio systems, PCs, the Internet, and smartphones, the 20s and 30s will see accelerated change, and things will be a major component of the new capabilities that will arise. In commercial circles, the term "Industry 4.0" has been coined to describe the impact that things will have. The next-wave industrial revolution will be based on the ubiquitous nature of things; our ability to measure and control them will be a defining characteristic of this development. We can now do this with unprecedented ease. IoT technology has developed at such a rapid pace that only our resistance to change is holding us back.

Multiple areas of our lives will be impacted by IoT: our shopping experience, vehicles, homes, cities, utilities, and logistics.

Personal

Wearables are impacting our lives in significant ways. Fitbit arguably now has the largest global repository of health information ever to exist. Lives have been saved by Fitbit devices providing simple, understandable data that allows users to engage with medical professionals in a more meaningful way.

Smart watches have enormous potential as a user interface; not for emails or any sort of data input, but for notifications and event monitoring. Your smart watch will allow you to receive alarms if you're approaching a danger, for instance, or to notify someone of your proximity. Lightweight, inexpensive watches will be popular in North America. Sophisticated, expensive watches will be popular in Asia.

Other wearables that will be important are devices integrated with our clothing. Shoes or socks that monitor our walking or running will be important, as will be clothes that monitor our activity and generate a notification if an "out of pattern" event occurs, such as a fall.

Vehicle

Automobiles now contain more computers than the average house. The most ubiquitous IoT technology will be associated with vehicle service events. Automobiles will be programmed with the users' details, and service arrangements will be approved via an SMS text to the owner's phone number in the vehicle's identity data record as it goes in for a service. Diagnostic detail will also be passed from the automobile when it enters the service center. Similarly, vehicles will provide more service details to vehicle owners via their smartphone. Trip details, fuel usage, and service requirements will be transmitted to the user on demand or on event. Increasingly, statistics on driverless episodes and driver competence will be collected and potentially made available.

Home Automation

It is now easy to control devices in our houses. Such devices will become more ubiquitous, and data management software will become available to provide us with a much richer environment in which to understand information such as power usage for heating and cooling. Common facilities will be systems that provide us with the capability to control temperature, lights, and door access from our smartphones. The need for robust identity management should be obvious.

Retail

Like it or not, retail will be a major user of things. Large department stores are already installing cellular and beacon technology designed to maintain a dialog with their regular customers and act as a promotion vehicle to attract new customers. With your permission, a store will welcome you to the shop, advise you of special promotions, and allow you to provide feedback on services. Without your permission, store management will be able to track your path through the store and learn information about your interests. It is likely that most customers will enable messaging in order to be advised of promotional offers that match their areas of interest.

Cities

There are many areas in which city infrastructure uses IoT technology, as shown in Table 7.2.

Table 7.2: IoT usage in city infrastructure

Usage	Description
Roads/Transport	We can expect better traffic control in the future with real-time monitoring of traffic density. City staff will use signage and personal navigators to route traffic around points of congestion. IoT technology will also facilitate monitoring of roadwork impact, so that corrective action can be taken.
Parking	One growing area of "things" usage will be parking. In-road devices will know how long a vehicle has been in one spot, so that the billing system can charge drivers accordingly.
Surveillance	Another area on its ascendancy is citizen surveillance. By installing cameras in known trouble spots, administrators are increasingly able to make our cities safer.

Utilities

The production, distribution, and sale of products and services by utilities is being massively affected by IoT technology. It is now inexpensive to remotely manage the delivery of water, gas, and electricity. Utilities' failure to take advantage of the resultant benefits means they are charging their customers too much; this is obviously unsustainable because customers will switch suppliers when the opportunity arises.

Logistics

IoT impacts logistics in multiple areas. As consumer electronic commerce continues to increase, there will be a need for more package tracking and receipt confirmation. The increasing interest in innovative "last mile" delivery mechanisms make this an interesting sector for IoT deployments. Trucking companies increasingly need to adopt IoT technology. Access to port terminals and hazardous goods management all require communication of data to or from things, be they RFID, NFC, Bluetooth, or Wi-Fi devices.

In the area of transport logistics, there are significant benefits to be achieved. For instance, automated notification of an "empty container return" to a container park would save supply chain customers significant costs.

Contributing Technologies

It is fortunate that IoT technology is developing at a time in which related services are becoming available. Not only are manufacturing economies of scale driving down the cost of devices, other technology developments are contributing to the economic viability of IoT installations.

Cloud

There are multiple areas in which the cloud contributes to IoT deployments. Data storage is one area to be addressed in any installation of IoT devices. In some cases, where data volumes are large, it makes sense to store data in the cloud where the requisite encryption is facilitated and the business continuity services offered by cloud service providers (CSPs), such as data backup and restore, can be leveraged.

It is arguably also easier to manage access to data in the cloud. With on-premises databases, there is a requirement to configure the access control settings for the database or put the data store on a protected subnet. In the cloud, user access can be restricted by the cloud service access control facility based on an attribute in the user's directory entry.

A CSP can also perform a useful communications task for companies with industrial computer installations with remote monitoring facilities. CSPs with multiple data centers can be used to collect data from remote monitoring points close to one facility and make it available via a data center close to the company's administration point.

Big Data Analysis

Sometimes devices produce a lot of data that needs to be analyzed either continuously or periodically for trends or to identify significant events. Here cloud-based services can be advantageous. Hadoop analysis and map-reduce functionality are easier to deploy in the cloud and can facilitate turning raw data into information for managers tasked with understanding IoT data and making appropriate management decisions.

Concerns

It's generally agreed among industry analysts that we are heading toward a catastrophe with IoT technology; it could be corporate but will more likely occur in the public sector. It will probably entail unauthorized access to sensitive data that is subsequently released to nefarious persons, or it may be a malicious attack on a control device resulting in inappropriate messages being sent to an industrial process. The result will be unprecedented regulation being imposed on IoT systems. It will be the classic "closing the gate after the horse has bolted" syndrome and will happen because:

- Those in authority in this technology space are abrogating their responsibility to understand and impose governance over IoT. This is most unfortunate because it does not need to happen: plenty of help in the form of information and tools is available, and there are enough people who know how to use them.

- Those with regulatory authority fail to develop regulation until they have to. This, too, is most unfortunate because we know what can go wrong, and we have the technology to stop things from going wrong. Industry is quite capable of working with government to ensure that regulation is sufficient and fit-for-purpose; waiting until there's a political expediency means regulation will likely be draconian and expensive.

But it's not all doom and gloom. There are some bright spots that we will come to soon.

Best Practices

There are a number of areas in which organizations should plan their IoT implementations to optimize their usefulness and avoid potential problems.

Data Management

Data from sensors must be securely collected and adequately protected in storage. The data communication channel must be managed, and appropriate notifications should be issued. For instance, for temperature measurements, periodic transmissions are adequate with only averages stored for any length of time. However, if a temperature reading is outside normal ranges, an alarm should be raised.

Depending on the sensitivity of the data, it might be necessary to digitally sign the transmission of data collected so that the receiver can be sure it originated at the prescribed sensor. Or the data might be encrypted to ensure that the message can't be intercepted and understood.

It is also necessary to define controls on data being written to corporate systems. If Web services are being used, the HTTP method(s) that can write—to a database, for instance—and the conditions placed on it, should be documented. For high-security environments, APIs should be used that define the data that can be passed through the interface and what can be done with it. For instance, a popular data transfer mechanism is an XML file using a signed SOAP message. If the message is not appropriately signed, it will not be actioned, and if the XML file does not use the prescribed tag names, the data will not be written to the protected repository.

Note: Enterprise data store interface protocols such as SQL or LDAP should not be deployed in a cross-boundary environment. If data is originating from a remote location, the use of an API is highly recommended. In this way, the appropriate API security, which insures the confidentiality and integrity of the data, and API management, which ensures that governance processes are observed, will be implemented. When it comes to actuators, it is most important to adequately restrict access to these devices. If a device can be controlled by an unauthorized person, a potential catastrophe is enabled.

Device Categorization

Device capability, management requirements, and security controls vary widely depending on their "category." A controller in an in-house production line has a different security profile from the HVAC thermostat. Data from the production management system has a different sensitivity than the research results from the latest pharmaceutical trials. Categorization will ensure appropriate treatment of access control to devices and data from devices. This, in turn, will ensure that IoT infrastructure is not over-engineered, which adds costs, or under-engineered, which could possibly expose the organization to unnecessary risk.

So, What Can Be Done?

While the level of complexity around IoT outstrips the knowledge of many CIOs, there are many tools and services available that obviate the need to understand the complexity. CIOs cannot be expected to understand the intricacies of potential devices and their interface capabilities. But there's help:

IoT Security Foundation

The IoT Security Foundation (IoTSF) was created by like-minded individuals who recognized early on the IoT catastrophe on the horizon. The basic tenet of the Foundation is that security must be designed into a solution, not tacked on later. This means that a number of things must be in place:

- A "best practices" approach is needed to help device designers adhere to basic principles that allow their devices to meet a base level of conformance; a process is also needed to allow for the identification, notification, and recertification of devices identified as deficient.

- Guidance is required on the security aspects of IoT APIs; no software programmer should be engaged to develop an API, or an application that interfaces with an API, without the associated guidelines being in place.

- A mechanism is needed to update IoT devices when a deficiency is discovered; for devices that are too small or low cost for this, a mechanism to retire them is required.

It also means that a way to control the appropriate conformance and testing of devices is required. A vehicle control computer has a vastly different risk profile from a home automation switch. It is necessary to define categories of devices and an associated profile of characteristics and conformance requirements. CIOs just need to make sure their devices are correctly categorized and the appropriate controls are established.

The nice thing about the IoTSF is it is an international association, so it is not controlled by any one jurisdiction, and it is also collaborative—no one is dictating the rules.

Kantara Initiative

Another initiative that has been around for several years now is the Kantara Initiative, which provides direction on, among other things, the responsible design and development of APIs. The Kantara Initiative has already done much of the heavy lifting by developing well-thought-out processes. In addition, sample code and assistance in conformance testing are available to members, which can save time and money in getting a product to market.

The focus is on tracking technology developments and staying ahead of the curve on developing best practices, particularly when it comes to leveraging identity information for the management of access to applications, data, and devices. Kantara has developed a "trust framework" to allow organizations to determine if, and how much, they will trust an identity attested to by another identity provider. The rules for approving and determining the reliance to be placed on a credentialing service, for instance, have been defined.

A strong focus for Kantara is the usability of applications that monitor devices and control access. By leveraging identity attributes, secure access to device data and device control capability is enabled. The User Managed Access (UMA) workgroup has published specifications for the development of user-focused solutions to allow users to collect and share data from "things" and to make it simple to do so. Interoperability testing is also supported. If providing device control and sharing data securely is not both secure and intuitive, it's not fit-for-purpose.

Members include companies such as CA Technologies, ForgeRock, and Radiant Logic, as well as government agencies such as the U.S. General Services Administration (GSA) and Australia's Digital Transformation Agency (DTA).

FIDO

The Fast IDentity Online (FIDO) alliance was formed to generate standards for authenticating devices. These can be any sort of fixed or mobile device, including smartphones. While smartphones are increasingly being supported by organizations as input devices, they do raise some issues. Enterprises need to know who is operating a device and, based on their identity, implement an appropriate level of access control. The FIDO Alliance assists by providing high-assurance access control at the device level that can assist in deploying an authentication environment, which will assert the owner's identity to a relying application. FIDO has worked in two areas:

- Password-less authentication via a high-assurance process such as facial recognition or fingerprint verification
- Two-factor authentication by using "something you have" attached to the input device

Many companies now support FIDO, including PayPal, Google, and Microsoft. The software stack is being built into smartphones and other devices, which makes FIDO the standard of choice for companies that want a high degree of assurance about who is using a device. It is likely that IoT devices that require high-assurance authentication will also embrace the standard.

A Reference Architecture

It is highly recommended that an organization establish an architecture for an IoT environment. The IoT architecture should also "plug in to" the enterprise architecture in the operating system, communications infrastructure, and data storage areas. A simple reference architecture should include the components shown in Figure 7.1.

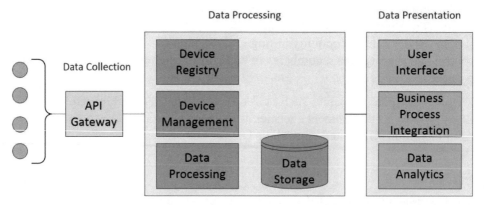

Figure 7.1: IoT reference architecture

API Gateway

APIs define the "rules of integration" for both collection and control devices. The API provides guidance to the construction of an interface from devices, so that each device can be validated and the information can be identified for data processing purposes. The API also provides management capabilities to allow the performance statistics, data throughput, and data characteristics to be properly reported and managed.

Device Registry

It is important that detail on the quantity and type of devices in the field is known and manageable. This should be achieved through a registration process that initiates the device and establishes any required encryption and interface configuration.

Device Management

The management of devices is similar to identity management. The repository must store the identifier and attributes of the device for access control purposes. If a device must be taken offline, this will generally occur via a device management function.

Data Processing

Data processing is the function that reads the raw data and performs the necessary transformation to make it usable within the company. In some cases, this will be simply writing the data to storage for post processing, while at other times it will require concatenation and trend detection. Data processing will generally include event monitoring and notification.

Data Storage

Storing data appropriately is an important function because there can be a lot of data to store. Cloud storage is increasingly popular because of the data quantities and the common requirement to conduct some form of big data analysis, which is facilitated by most CSPs.

User Interface

The user interface varies. It might be a simple report of collected data, or it might be a supervisory control and data acquisition (SCADA) screen to control a device that is part of a process. It is important that this component of the architecture be interfaced to the company's identity and access management facility to ensure that all access is appropriate, and properly managed.

Business Process Integration

For device monitoring that is part of a business process, integration of the appropriate data into the process is important. In some cases, this integration will be manual—that is, operations personnel will monitor the data stream. In other cases, the integration will be automated, in which case some form of data processing will identify meaningful events and notify the appropriate business process.

Data Analytics

An important component of an IoT integration project is to ensure that the appropriate analytics are generated and displayed. This might be via a dashboard or through integration into the organization's monitoring and control infrastructure.

Philosophy of IoT

This is an appropriate point to stop and reflect for a moment on another aspect of IoT that sometimes gets forgotten in the euphoria of technological advances. There are multiple ways in which IoT will affect society. It's not only the new capabilities that it opens up, or the truly innovative solutions that we will marvel at when they are released. IoT will also open up exciting discussions about data ownership, and it will be the instigator of altruistic initiatives that will have truly life-changing consequences for those affected. Identity management is at the core of these discussions.

If a Fitbit collects information about a person's health, the number of steps they have taken, their pulse rate, and sleeping patterns, who owns the data? No doubt the initial response will be "the user." But what about the aggregated data that Fitbit stores? What if this could be combined with data from the US Centers for Disease Control and Prevention to pinpoint an outbreak of an epidemic, or contribute to the deployment of treatment resources. Now who owns the data?

What about gas wells? What if sensors start to detect harmful gases or groundwater contamination? Is this private or public information? How do we want our regulators to respond? When do we want this to occur: after a catastrophe or now?

Possibly the time has come for proactive legislation. We should not have to wait for our elected officials to react to an IoT situation. There are enough professionals who know what can go wrong; we just need to advise our politicians as to what we want.

This has implications for organizations that are installing measurement and control devices. The model to monetize such investments is changing. Collaboration, potentially with competitors, will likely be the hallmark of future large-scale IoT initiatives.

As IT professionals, we have the opportunity to contribute to shaping the impact of IoT on society. Let's not shirk this responsibility.

Next Steps

So, how should organizations exploit this potential? What can be done to make sure companies don't miss the opportunities that arise?

Step 1: Strategy Development

The most important step in exploiting IoT is developing a strategy. Without this step, there will be no appreciation of the potential of IoT to assist the organization and therefore no development of competitive advantage based on the potential of "things" to improve business processes.

Worse still, some business units within the organization might decide to "go it alone" and develop IoT facilities without implementing the proper controls or a plan for wider development in the company. This is dangerous because there will be no management oversight of interfaces that are developed, resulting in exposure of the company to unnecessary risk and potential damage to corporate infrastructure and potentially the community.

Ideally IoT integration should be within the controls established for technology integration in the corporation's enterprise architecture. IoT devices should be addressed at the technology level to give business units guidance on supported device types, so that there are not a plethora of different devices deployed within the organization. At the application level, APIs for device integration should be determined with management and security requirements stipulated. At the information level, the device integration should be addressed with direction given for database interfaces and data management controls. At the business level, the processes impacted by IoT devices should be determined with consideration given to wider deployment of IoT technology or sharing of IoT data with a wider audience.

Interfaces to the identity management and access control facilities should be addressed at the information architecture level.

Strategy must, by definition, include an environmental scan that determines the current situation. This will include documenting current capabilities and desired goals, and possibly a SWOT analysis to identify the weaknesses to be overcome and the opportunities to be exploited.

This must include a definition of how IoT will integrate with the IdM environment.

Step 2: Capability Development

There's little point in developing a strategy if there's no capability to put it into action. Organizations might have IoT expertise on staff— particularly if they are managing a production environment, these staff should investigate the opportunity to extend their manufacturing system to provide better data or controls to business unit personnel. In the event that there is no in-house expertise, it will need to be brought in or developed. In the event that a system integrator is engaged to deploy an IoT system, reliance on the supplier might well be the best approach, but this must be done within the constraints of the company's policy and practices. It is important to ask the right questions, so that the organization's commercial integrity and intellectual property are protected.

Step 3: Infrastructure Deployment

The deployment step is a standard project management exercise:

- Plan—investigate options and develop a project plan.
- Design a solution—this will include understanding the business unit requirements and documenting the desired outcomes.
- Deploy the technology—this will include an interface to the organization's IAM environment to manage access controls.
- Test, both functionality and volume, to ensure that the project deliverables meet the customer requirements and expectations.
- Transition to operations—once the acceptance testing has been completed, the infrastructure transitions to maintenance. This may be in house or outsourced.

Step 4: Business Process Integration

Once the project is completed and the IoT environment is generating a data stream and providing control capabilities, the next step is to integrate the IoT system into the business. This could be simply training business unit staff on the system capabilities. In other cases, the IoT data feeds will need to be integrated with business system databases, and the ability to control processes integrated with business systems. Identity management that provides access control to data and devices will be paramount.

Conclusion

IoT has already had a significant impact on our lives and will continue to do so. Governments have an unprecedented ability to manage the built environment to make our commutes easier, infrastructure maintenance cheaper, and our cities safer. Companies have the ability to significantly change business processes and develop competitive advantage. And we all have the opportunity to manage our home environments to increase comfort and decrease costs.

It is no longer a question as to if IoT will impact government, companies. and the public. Now it is just a question of how big the impact will be.

The answer to this question, in many ways, depends upon how we manage identity data. If we manage it appropriately to ensure the right people have the right access to the right devices at the right time, the benefit has the potential to be great. We will be able to increasingly understand and manage our environment to the betterment of society.

If we fail to "get it right," or if we fail to educate the influencers and those in authority, the impact might be far greater than we ever imagined and far more disastrous.

Use Case: Building Management

Scenario	Property Management Company has a 20-story building with 15 commercial tenants in the central business district of a city. Tenants often complain that their areas are too cool in the morning and too hot on sunny days during the winter, and too hot in the morning and too cool in the afternoons during summer. The HVAC consultants have advised implementing a software upgrade that uses weather forecast information to manage HVAC settings and will provide an estimated 15% in energy savings. A wall-mounted thermometer in each zone will need to be installed.
Strategy	An analysis of the potential financial benefits of improving the building HVAC controls has indicated that the annual building energy cost, for heating in the winter and air conditioning in the summer, is $110,000 per year. Wall-mount temperature sensors are now available for $80 each; there are five zones per floor. The cost to upgrade the HVAC software and integrate the new sensors is $50,000. If a 15% energy savings can be achieved, the five-year net present value (NPV) is $135,000, with a three-year payback.
Solution	Property Management Company decided to place the temperature sensors and upgrade the HVAC management software but at the same time place proximity sensors for intrusion detection and event monitoring. A premium service will be offered to tenants, which will initiate an alarm when after-hours access is detected.

Q & A

Q. Must a company rely on their operational technology supplier for sensors and actuators? What if the supplier does not allow low-cost devices to be attached to their systems?

A. For a long time, industrial computer system suppliers have engaged in monopolistic pricing, requiring customers to purchase from them all devices they deploy. With the rapid reduction in the price and capability of sensors and actuators, this is no longer a viable business practice, and vendors are coming under pressure to support the connection of third-party devices to their equipment. Vendors should be requested to provide a list of "approved" third-party devices that will allow customers to maintain the quality of their systems but at the same time improve the financial justification of extending their current systems or replacing them with an alternative solution.

Any new system acquisition should stipulate that support of standards is an evaluation criterion.

Q. What if business units are not asking for data from, or access to, sensors or actuators; does this mean IoT is not needed?

A. No. It usually means that they have not been introduced to the possibilities. Appreciation of the benefits of IoT is a bit of a cultural shift that business units might need help to understand. A first step is to hold awareness workshops, with business unit staff, to talk about the possibilities and get their feedback.

Sometimes there will be no viable opportunities, whereas in other cases there will be several. It would be a shame to miss an opportunity to develop innovative and beneficial solutions that can drive competitive advantage.

If nothing else, it will strengthen the relationship between IT and the business units.

Q. What if a company does not have any devices, either sensors or controllers, at the moment? Is it still recommended that a project be initiated to consider deployment of IoT?

A. Absolutely.

It is likely that deployment of IoT equipment was not considered before because it was not economically viable. With the reduction in device costs, it is time to consider the opportunities that this technology can afford. For instance, if data from the production floor is currently being compiled and communicated manually, a better solution is to summarize it and report in real time in the future without the cost of manual intervention. It is unlikely that such a project would fail an economic justification, and it just might significantly enhance the sales effort.

Chapter 8

A Word About Industrial Computer Systems

The previous chapter discussed Internet of Things (IoT) and its impact on technology and identity management practices. IoT is also having a significant effect on industrial computer systems (ICSs). Companies that used to pay over $1,000 per device can now buy ICS devices for less than $100 each. Changes of that magnitude alter the entire paradigm for companies with ICS installations. Not only can they afford many more sensors and actuators, their maintenance regime may change, possibly from a preventative maintenance to an obsolescence strategy. Additionally, we are seeing impressive and innovative software that allows the control and sharing of IoT data based on attributes in a staff member's identity record.

There's another trend that's impacting industrial computer systems: in many industries a common practice has been to separate operational technology (OT) networks from the company's administrative networks that the IT department maintains. This has meant that OT networks have not been able to benefit from the advances in security protection that have occurred over the past few years in IT. For instance, many OT environments can't access their corporate identity and access management (IAM) environments to protect their ICS installations.

Now is the time for any company that is using computers for discrete or process control applications to consider industry trends in the IoT sector. Jack Welch[1] famously said, "If there's more change happening outside your business than inside, the end is near." That's the case in many manufacturing businesses where the likelihood of digital disruption is high.

The good news is, there's no impediment to change; the technology now exists, and the benefits are economically justifiable. In other words, the time is now to make significant changes to ICS installations and improve their integration with identity management environments.

---

[1] Former CEO of General Electric

Market Definition

An OT system is any system that is used to monitor or control a production or distribution system. It could be a manufacturing process that controls bottles as they are filled, an oil refinery that controls the cracking tower in the refining of petroleum products, or electricity grids that manage the generation and distribution of electricity to customers.

The sector can be segmented into discrete manufacturing, which typically uses binary measurement and actuators, and continuous process control systems, where measuring levels and controlling flows is important. In many cases, the control occurs at remote sites that are often in a "lights out" (i.e., unmanned) environment. Device control is typically placed close to the process being monitored or controlled by a programmable logic controller (PLC). A final component is often a supervisory control and data acquisition (SCADA) system that provides a graphical interface to system operators, which allows them to monitor and control the process under management. Figure 8.1 shows a typical SCADA configuration.

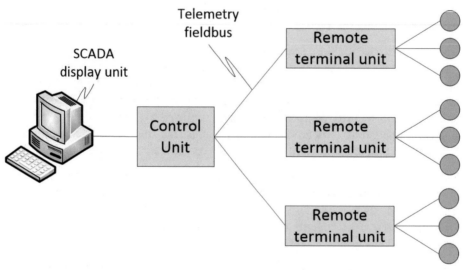

Figure 8.1: Typical SCADA configuration

The selection of communication mechanisms is wide, and will depend upon the distribution of the process under control. For a local manufacturing system, Ethernet is typically the chosen transport medium. If the process is remote, the selection of communication technology will be guided by these factors:

- Availability of communication—is wired or wireless communication available at the site, or does the company need to install its own communication technology?

- Volume and velocity—how much data will be collected, and how fast does data collection need to be?

- Regulation—is the industry regulated, either by the government or industry (e.g., electricity distribution), or can the company decide the mechanism it wants to employ?

In many cases, the industry will dictate the communication mechanism to be used. A common communication protocol is Message Queuing Telemetry Transport (MQTT), but this is only appropriate on fast communication channels. In remote locations that rely on telemetry installations, a Modbus variant may be more appropriate. In the electrical industry, Distributed Network Protocol (DNP3) is often used.

Managing these entities and their access to the network is not trivial. In sensitive environments, it is a good idea to encrypt/digitally sign communication from devices, but poor communication channels make this a challenge. It means that real-time management of keys is probably not realistic; periodic key rotation at maintenance times is probably best.

Legacy Scenarios

The current state of many OT installations is characterized by isolated networks and a strong reliance on system vendors.

Isolated Networks

In many organizations, OT systems are isolated from the IT systems. The often-stated reason is for "security," but upon closer examination, this argument is hard to support. There are better methods of implementing security by leveraging the organization's identity management infrastructure to enable a strong access control system to be deployed. The isolation of the OT network from the IT network makes this difficult.

In many ways, the isolation of OT networks has promulgated poor security practices. There tends to be a reliance on this isolation to relax account permissions. Many control rooms rely on generic logins because of the physical access control mechanisms that are in place. In situations where there are individual logins, there is an administrative overhead with a heavy reliance on manual intervention for account provisioning and de-provisioning because there is no connection to the company's IdM system in order to automate provisioning. The result is:

- No four-eyes control[2]—a single administrator can usually establish accounts.

- Orphaned accounts—poor de-provisioning practices

- No two-factor authentication (2FA)—an inability to access the corporate identity store makes 2FA more difficult, so it does not happen; this is unfortunate because multi-factor authentication is an important tool in the deployment of a secure access control environment.

Note: In some industries (e.g., electricity distribution), regulation precludes the integration of IT and OT networks, and an "air gap" will need to be maintained between the two networks. But even in these scenarios, there are some interesting technologies that should be considered to alleviate poor practices on the OT side.

Long In-service Times

OT systems have longevity, they are expensive to deploy, and vendors do not upgrade their technology at the same frequency as IT vendors, so they do not have the refresh rates of IT systems. Typical in-service times are 15 years with 30 years not uncommon. The result is that OT systems are not regularly upgraded to new operating systems and are generally not running on up-to-date patched OSs. Many industrial systems are running on Windows 7, and some are still on Windows 95.

Release Management

The long in-service times also result in an "if-it's-not-broken-don't-fix-it" syndrome when it comes to releasing new versions of control system software to fix bugs and to upgrade the system to the latest operating system software and apply security patches.

Rather than risking a system outage with a software upgrade, the tendency is to "do nothing." The logic goes like this: there might be an incompatibility between the new operating system and the control system that we don't identify during system testing, and there is the possibility that the control system could go down,

---

[2] Four-eyes control recognizes that opportunity for corrupt practices reduces dramatically when more than one person must authorize a transaction.

creating significant cost and embarrassment; therefore, we'll do nothing. The do-nothing approach is further justified by the savings in operational costs by not deploying resources.

> As a young manager, I was put in charge of a telephone switching center as a component of my management development program.
>
> Part of the business continuity procedure was a quarterly trial of the electrical generator, during which time the switching center was disconnected from the grid and operated on the backup power unit. I asked one of my staff when the last generator test was conducted, to which he replied "it never has been."
>
> It was with some trepidation that we completed the trial.

If a proper risk assessment was conducted, the fallacy of such logic would be evident. Unfortunately, too many managers are willing to turn a blind eye with the confidence that they can feign "lack of knowledge" if a compromise should occur on an unpatched or an out-of-support operating system. Given that company directors are increasingly being held to account for errors in their domain, regardless of the cause, this is a dangerous approach to take. It's particularly inappropriate since sophisticated services that make a robust software release methodology easy and inexpensive to deploy are available in the cloud. Cloud service providers now offer and maintain full test environments that enable proper regression testing to be undertaken for a new release, or operating system upgrade.

One IAM issue that does affect the test regime is the necessity to anonymize data used for testing. A test directory should not include identity records of actual people, be they staff, business partners, or customers.

Vendor Reliance

Because of the technical nature of OT systems, companies tend to rely on vendor "specialists" to design and sometimes manage their solutions. Companies rely on them to know the industry regulation and to design compliant systems. Once the system is installed, vendors often maintain a "back door" account to be able to remotely manage the system. Often this account is of a generic nature and, while passwords are typically rotated, there is no effective control on which individual in the vendor organization accessed and made changes to a system. At the least, each staff member from the vendor organization should have their own identity record within the organization's IdP. Better still, federated authentication should be put in place, which relies on the vendor's IdP for login purposes. This will require an investigation of the vendor's registration process and for agreement to be reached on the most appropriate access control mechanism to be deployed.

Steps to a Future Scenario

To exploit the opportunities that an integrated OT/IT approach can afford, it is important that industrial organizations position themselves to take advantage of industry trends. There is a growing awareness that technology on the IT side has much to offer operational networks. To exploit these technology trends, it is necessary to review current OT policy and procedures and make changes that remove old prejudices and develop operational efficiencies that strengthen the company's capabilities to compete in the digital economy. If this can be achieved, the prize is unprecedented business enablement: business partners will be able to view product availability, customers will be able to place custom-designed orders, freight companies will be able to provide better package tracking, and utilities will be able to exploit spot pricing. To deny a company this business potential under the guise of "network security" is a great shame.

So how should this be achieved?

First, all companies, except those that are unable to do so from a regulatory point of view, should define the degree to which OT networks and IT networks can be integrated. Segmentation of the networks should be maintained, either via firewall technology or one-way gateways, but the OT system should be able to benefit from the security improvements that are now available in the IT environment—in particular, the IdP service.

Second, access control should be based on individual accounts that enable system interaction to be tracked to individuals, and the provisioning system should ensure that a staff member's access is removed when they leave the organization. It also means that, to the degree possible, partner (e.g., vendor) access should use mechanisms such as federated authentication, whereby access is granted based on the vendor's identity provider service.

Third, companies should explore opportunities for business processes to be integrated with ICSs. Workshops should be held with appropriate business units to determine whether ICS data or device control facilities would facilitate the business processes of any of the lines of business. This will identify any business process that can benefit from integration with the ICSs to provide them operational data or to control facilities that drive business enablement.

Note: It is likely that a cultural change will be required to effectively integrate OT and IT environments. OT personnel have traditionally enjoyed their isolation from IT services and corporate governance, and sometimes consider themselves "special" and outside normal business practices. They may even use safety concerns to avoid discussion of integration. This is to be anticipated and countered with a focus on current IT security capabilities.

Trends

Several trends associated with OT should be considered.

From Isolation to Integration

As we have seen, there are significant benefits on the OT side if there is a degree of integration with the IT infrastructure. The level of integration that 1) is allowable and 2) makes sense must be determined.

While in the past isolation between networks has been used to give an aura of security, the notion that isolation implies security no longer holds true. The security shortcomings of an isolated OT network—use of generic accounts because there's no access to identity control data stores, poor management of system access for contractors because of the lack of administrative assistance, and use of unregulated back-door accounts for vendors because federation is too difficult—all raise the risk profile of the industrial computer system network.

However, integration must be viewed through the prism of common sense and regulatory controls. An integration strategy based on a review of industry guidelines is appropriate. In OT implementations, a three-level classification system is often proposed[3]. Table 8.1 shows this classification system.

---

[3] Agence Nationale de la Sécurité des Systèmes d'Information (ANSSI) best-practice guidelines

Table 8.1: Security classification system for OT networks

Class	Description
Class 1—low-sensitivity networks	These are networks with applications that have little public impact in the case of a breach or system failure. Manufacturing applications that pose no public danger in the event of disaster are a case in point. These types of installations should be integrated with information systems to enable access control based on the organization's identity store and to enable sharing of data, as appropriate, with other personnel in the company. This is virtually impossible without access to the corporate IT network.
Class 2—medium-sensitivity networks	These networks incorporate applications that have a potentially significant societal impact should a disaster strike. For instance, a mining operation with the potential for large-scale pollution if a waste-water release valve is inappropriately operated could pose such a threat. In this instance, it is important that access to the control system be adequately protected. Integration between the OT and IT systems should be implemented, with adequate control to secure the OT control system. This will allow real-time access to identity repositories for access control purposes but still provide a degree of separation between the two networks. This will ensure, for instance, that a recently dismissed employee will no longer be able to gain access to the control room because the HR system would have disabled their AD account. Class 2 networks should maintain documentation of the safeguards they have put in place, and the company should conduct periodic audits.

Class 3—high-sensitivity networks	In this instance, there is significant safety risk should a disaster strike or a security breach occur. A railway switch management system is a case in point. Should the control system for the railway switch system be compromised, significant risk to public safety may be the result.
	It is not a requirement that all Class 3 networks be isolated. There are good reasons for integration between switch control operational networks and IT networks, not the least of which is the improved access control that ensues. For instance, with access to the rostering system, control room access can be restricted to rostered-on staff; other staff would require an online approval before access is granted. Other benefits, such as better analysis of network operations and improved customer service, are also enabled.
	In some cases, regulatory control mandates isolation between OT and IT networks (e.g., electricity grid control systems), in which case there are no options, and other mechanisms for keeping access control systems current and effective are required.
	Class 3 networks require external compliance audits to be performed, typically by a relevant government-appointed agency.

Classification of a network is often somewhat arbitrary. Typically, it is up to the company that owns the infrastructure to substantiate and document the classification decision.

Isolation mechanisms that are appropriate for networks with sensitive applications include technology solutions such as:

- Firewalls and routers that permit traffic flow based on predefined policies; these devices typically use IP address segmentation or group memberships for access control.

- Gateways that typically provide a finer-grained access control based on a user's individual attributes

- API gateways that apply sophisticated controls to allow access only to appropriately formed requests that adhere to the programming interface requirements

- Uni-directional gateways that will allow a flow of data from the OT network but not the other way (except at a specified time for a specified duration, if so allowed)

The strategy that an organization will follow should involve a review of potential solutions against a realistic analysis of corporate and industry requirements.

From Proprietary to Open Standards

In the past, vendors of operational technology developed their own systems that were often incompatible with systems from competitors. This was in part a natural outcome of the state of the industry—each company was developing innovative technology, and there was not much opportunity to collaborate—and in part due to a "lock-in" strategy to ensure ongoing sales from customers who wanted system extensions. This is no longer a tenable strategy because of the development of standards and the dramatic decrease in costs of connected devices. It is now possible to purchase sensor and actuator devices at a fraction of what they cost a decade ago. Regulation is also playing a part, as regulatory agencies stipulate industry-standard protocols to be used for certain highly sensitive deployments, such as electricity grid applications.

This means that, for industrial applications, vendors are being called upon to concentrate their development effort on aspects of their solutions and service offerings that differentiate them from their competition. Focusing on the user experience is one area in which this can occur. It is increasingly important that an operator be able to intuitively understand how devices are configured, and be able to optimize their infrastructure deployments. For instance, if it is desired to change the sampling rate on a thermometer to optimize data storage, this should be something an operator can do without the vendor's involvement.

Another area of product extension is the adoption of artificial intelligence (AI) to configure changes to a system to optimize its operation, or to generate an alert in the event that operator changes would harm the system.

From Private to Cloud Infrastructure

The decision to deploy industrial control systems on cloud infrastructure is not trivial. Several issues must be addressed, as shown in Table 8.2, which will determine the degree to which the cloud can be leveraged.

Table 8.2: Benefits and dangers of the cloud

Cloud Benefits	Operating on up-to-date, patched infrastructure is one of the biggest benefits of leveraging cloud infrastructure for OT deployments. This is a major security benefit. Organizations that do not have the in-house capability to keep their infrastructure on current operating system versions should seriously consider such a move.
	Maintaining a software release strategy with full regression testing is often easier in a cloud environment because of the ease with which containerized software can be moved around and deployed on multiple systems and the ability to conduct full regression testing.
	In addition, cloud storage is a major benefit. The ability to expand storage capacity instantaneously and have the CSP provide a tailored backup solution is a strong incentive. If there is a need for big data analysis to identify trends in collected data, or to analyze logs, there's another imperative for the cloud; most CSPs provide Hadoop services and map-reduce functionality.
Cloud Dangers	Security is often cited as a reason to not deploy on cloud services, but this may not be a valid reason. CSPs can now provide an environment that will suit the most stringent of requirements, usually in excess of the security associated with on-premises data centers. However, part of selecting a CSP is to ensure that it meets the stipulated levels of physical and logical access protection.
	Network latency is also a very real issue, particularly for instances in which sub-second control signals are required. However, implementations with such stringent limitations typically operate with PLCs located near the sensor and actuator devices. This provides fast response times for the control and data acquisition devices while allowing management systems to be located in the cloud where network latency is typically less of a concern.

It is worthwhile to reflect on another oft-cited reason for staying in the corporate data center: susceptibility to loss of service resulting from a critical event. For instance, "What if the CSP has a service outage and stops our manufacturing process?" Again, a CSP typically provides a more reliable service than many corporate data centres. While CSPs in the past have typically been unwilling to take on the liability of potentially stopping a production line, most suppliers are willing to put their SLAs in writing in order to allow potential customers to make an informed decision. All too often, corporate data center audits find issues such as failed disks in a stripe set, backup generators without a regular test regime, or redundant network connections running through common cable ducts—all issues that a CSP would not tolerate.

Providing an IdM solution in the cloud is a requirement for cloud migration of IoT. It is not acceptable to require authentication requests to traverse the corporate firewall to access the company's on-premises identity provider service. This means that an IdP must be made available on cloud services (see chapter 5 for more detail).

Considerations

Companies that have an OT requirement should consider conducting regular reviews in the following areas.

Define Level of Integration

As noted above, determining the level of integration with IT systems is arguably the most important decision to be made when deploying an OT installation. Integration will enable the OT network to leverage security controls that are available on the information security networks. Access to an up-to-date identity repository for access control decisions based on identity attributes is generally considered most important. The ability to deploy two-factor authentication facilities based on possession of a device such as a smartphone is enabled via such integration; use of a biometric credential such as a fingerprint or facial recognition template is also facilitated by access to an identity directory service. Integration also facilitates the exploitation of facilities such as privileged account management services for access to operational network systems and secure sharing of operational data.

Review Communication Requirements

The rapid development of hacker technology holds a special threat for OT networks. The sophistication of hacker tools can make networks, previously thought secure, vulnerable to "man-in-the-middle" attacks whereby a rogue entity spoofs a trusted device. Instituting digital signing-on communication between remote terminal units and control systems is highly advisable. Encryption should also be considered.

In one instance, it was found that a remote controller was communicating back to the database server via a service account. The username and password for the account were hard-coded in the server-side API in clear text.

Sometimes such protection is difficult. For instance, if the fieldbus connections to remote terminal units are over poor-quality telemetry circuits, higher-level communication protocols are difficult to implement. Remote management of encryption keys can also be difficult, decreasing the likelihood that encryption keys will be rotated. This can represent another attack vector in some circumstances.

Develop a Cloud Services Strategy

A cloud strategy is essential for any network, not just operational networks. However, operational networks are potentially the most likely to benefit from cloud deployments. Access to up-to-date and fully patched systems, with auto-scaling and backed-up storage, as well as access to facilities such big-data analysis, offer a compelling argument.

This means that OT network planning must develop a strategy to manage migration to the cloud. This strategy should be aligned with the corporate enterprise architecture. (See chapter 5 for more detail on cloud issues.)

Develop a BYOD Strategy

There are some distinct advantages to the support of mobile devices within an OT environment. A characteristic of the OT deployments is the 24 × 7 staffing requirements and, sometimes, hostile environments. Mobile devices provide advantages in such situations by adding a degree of flexibility to system monitoring and operation. If an operator does not have to be physically present, but available if need be, a smartphone or tablet is ideal because the staff member can be performing other productive work and can connect to the OT system via a mobile phone app or via a 2FA protected website to provide management, if necessary.

Another major benefit associated with tablets is the touchscreen. Many SCADA systems employ a graphic management screen, or mimic diagram, that is ideally suited to touchscreen technology. By displaying the process under control on a touchscreen, the user can select the sensor or actuator of concern and even make adjustments to the process under control via a wheel, dial, or switch that is graphically depicted on the screen.

If the decision is made that mobile devices are to be used, the next question should be "corporate device or user-owned device?" While there is usually no right or wrong answer, for most OT operations a user-owned device would generally not be satisfactory. The advantage of a corporate device is the complete organizational control that can be exerted over the device. This means that a high degree of security can be built into the mobile device app that accesses the corporate application. Disadvantages of using a corporate device are that users must carry a second device, which will be considered an annoyance; and capital must be allocated to purchase corporate devices.

The BYOD approach removes these two disadvantages but adds the necessity to reach an agreement with staff on the use of their own equipment. This will typically take the form of placing a "container" on their device over which the company has control—that is, the device can be wiped if the user leaves the company or loses the device. (See chapter 6 for more detail.)

Note: In some cases, a company-supplied "on-call" device will be deployed that rotates between on-call staff who are rostered on to cover out-of-business hours. In this instance, it is important to require staff to login individually and not use a generic "on-call" account. This will help enable responsibility to be appropriately assigned. It also allows attributes such as a staff member's training credential on a machine to be checked before granting access.

Investigate Authorization

The uptake in authorization services has a lot to offer OT deployments. Authorization provides the ability to perform fine-grained access control where a number of attributes—both the requestor's attributes, from the IdP, and context attributes such as time of day—are evaluated against a common policy set to determine whether or not a user will be granted access. For instance, access can be managed according to the user's job function, the type of device being used, and the time of day.

A risk management approach, whereby an access request made via an on-premises PC during business hours, would be evaluated differently from an access late at night from a mobile device, is recommended.

Such an authorization system has much to offer OT systems. For instance, access to the process control SCADA system can be restricted to only those with an endorsement in their identity record indicating that they have demonstrated the requisite proficiency on the system to which access has been requested.

Define API Management Guidelines

For OT applications that use APIs to control data flow from sensors, both API security and the API management guidelines need to be defined. For instance, in a Web services environment, the action of HTTP methods should be documented; guidance on which HTTP methods can be used to write to a database, and under what conditions, should be provided.

For control purposes, access to the organization's IdP can enable policy-based access control. For instance, access to a manufacturing process can be limited to employees in the manufacturing operations work group. If digital signing is to be invoked, a definition of the key management regime is required, and the logging and audit requirement must also be specified.

ISA-95

Readers should be aware of the ISA-95[4] regulatory guidelines for operational technology solutions in manufacturing. It is recommended that six components, shown in Table 8.3, be analyzed to complete a solution design.

Table 8.3: Components of an operational technology solution

Component	Description
Equipment	An inventory of the equipment used is required. This data will typically be held in an asset database that will facilitate maintenance schedules and training requirements. Each piece of equipment will be identified and its attributes (e.g., description, class, weight, capacity) recorded. A pictorial diagram of the equipment's position in the process under control will often be included.
Material	The material required for a process will be documented. This will include raw material that is required for the process, intermediary material (i.e., work in process), and the final products.
Personnel	A personnel inventory is recommended, which defines for each machine the personnel requirements and the staff that meet each requirement. This inventory should be integrated with the organization's identity data store, where the attributes should be recorded. Access to the organization's roster allows control of authority to machines and equipment.

---

[4] ANSI/ISA-95 is an international standard that provides guidance on interfacing control systems to enterprise systems.

Component	Description *Table 8.3 continued*
Process	By dividing a process into "cells," the machine and staffing requirements can be effectively managed. For instance, there may be a build cell and a packaging cell. Treating them separately will ensure that appropriate and sufficient staff, as well as other required resources, are available to allow the process to operate effectively.
Product	The product definition describes the components of a product and any process requirements. This ensures that the right material can be planned and the necessary equipment made available to build sufficient product volumes.
Schedule	The schedule defines the allocation of resources to a particular build. By knowing the quantity to be produced, the material, personnel, and process component resources can be used to schedule the work necessary to meet production requirements.

ISA-95 provides a useful model for the analysis and design of manufacturing systems. It can be used to identify touch points with business processes within an organization in order to manage a manufacturing process.

Conclusion

Identity and access management has significant ability to influence the development of an organization's industrial computer system environment. As companies increasingly integrate their OT and IT environments, a major driver is the ability for the IT environment to satisfy the operational computing environment.

A major impetus to such integration is coming from the disruptive technology surrounding sensors and actuators. The price reduction of such devices makes it advantageous to re-evaluate corporate approaches to OT systems.

Another driver is the desire to establish common governance across both environments so that corporate policy is observed. With significant advances occurring in the IT sector, there's a growing desire to leverage these developments in the OT space.

Identity management enables access control to data from sensors, the ability to share it appropriately with others in the organization, and the ability to manage access to devices that control operational processes within the company.

Use Case: Railway Management

Scenario	Train Administration Services in Big City Railroad Limited produces a monthly report on a variety of statistics, such as the number of passenger miles, passenger numbers by rail segment by hour and by each day or for the week, signals passed at danger (SPADs), and rail car maintenance levels. This data is all transposed from various reports that are prepared manually by train operations staff.
Strategy	The desire is to collect data automatically from train operations systems. Train ops maintains an OT network that is isolated from Railroad's IT systems. Passenger numbers are available from the Station Infrastructure System that monitors turnstiles; SPADs are available from the Network Control System; and miles travelled, by car, is available via a minor modification to the network control SCADA system. Access is restricted to train operations management staff. A manually maintained access control list is used to control access to operational systems.
Solution	The solution involved the installation of a unidirectional firewall that maintains invisibility of the OT network from Big City Railroad's administration but allows the appropriate OT systems to write data to the train management data warehouse. The monthly reports can then be compiled automatically from the operational data that is stored in the data warehouse. In addition, a 10-minute flow reversal each day allows the company's IdP data to be copied to the OT network for access control purposes.

Q & A

Q. One of the benefits of keeping an OT network separate from an IT network is that it ensures that contractors gain access to systems on the OT network but not to corporate systems on the IT network. Is this not a good reason for maintaining isolation between the two networks?

A. No. An identity management system is well capable of logically segmenting the access requirements of systems regardless of their user base. A good identity management system will enable provisioning into systems based on the rules established for provisioning, and in accordance with the approval workflows that have been established. This means that a contractor will only be provisioned into the operational systems they require to complete their job duties, and they will only get access rights when the person responsible for granting access rights approves their access. Contractors will not be allowed access to corporate administrative systems since no one will approve their access.

One issue to avoid is the use of generic contractor accounts. In some companies, a single generic account is established for all contractors. This is a poor practice because it eliminates the ability to audit access and assign responsibility to individuals. It also eliminates the possibility to leverage user data for other purposes, such as to prefill forms, or leverage other identity management capabilities.

Q. If an OT network is geographically remote from the company's administrative network, what's the point of integration? It will be a different set of users, different network infrastructure, and different systems to which they need access.

A. While the work activity of an OT person and an administrative person is very different, there are common administrative processes and an overarching governance model. For these reasons, an integrated infrastructure should be considered. For instance, it is unlikely that a separate HR system will be in place for contractors, or that a separate finance system is used for the OT side of the business. This means that the central administrative systems need to be leveraged as authoritative sources of identity and financial information in order to manage system access and other user attributes.

Q. Who should be responsible for managing the access rights to data from remote sensors or access control to actuators?

A. Business units should determine and manage access to data collected from operational systems and should determine who should access control devices.

IT should enable the access to happen and provide the systems for secure sharing of collected data. IT has a role to educate business unit personnel in the possibilities and then to deploy the necessary systems for business unit enablement.

Chapter 9

Sharing Securely: How to Cope

It comes as a surprise to some business people I talk to that they need to accommodate data sharing. "No" is sometimes their approach: "We don't want to share data because it becomes more insecure; we want to protect it and limit data sharing." You can't argue with the logic "the more people who can access protected data, the harder it is to protect." But it reminds me of the famous comedy sketch in which the hospital with no patients had the best KPIs: the lowest cost base and the shortest wait times. To not share data severely hinders the ability of an organization to do business. Organizations consist of people, and people need to share information in order to perform their job responsibilities.

Secure information sharing is a requirement of business today. Organizations can no longer secure the corporate network and pretend the company's intellectual property and sensitive information is safe from malicious attacks or inadvertent loss. The network perimeter is so porous now that relying on firewalls and network edge devices is no longer tenable. Managers face an overwhelming amount of information, both structured and unstructured, and making efficient use of this data securely is becoming increasingly nuanced.

There is an increasing need to share data, not just within the organization but with business partners as well as customers. In the digital business, this increased communication has significant benefits to each line of business, improving efficiency and reducing costs. This data sharing also extends to business partners up and down the supply chain.

But there are increasingly more proficient solutions. As network solutions have become more and more incapable of providing robust data loss protection, secure data sharing solutions have become more competent in providing sophisticated solutions that organizations can use to protect themselves as they embrace data sharing—securely.

So organizational efficiency, cost reductions, and revenues improve as data is shared. But in order to support business processes, an organization must provide access to data that might be sensitive, so it is important that cybersecurity requirements are adequately observed. Determining the balance between security and business efficiency in the adoption of new technology is the task at hand.

The Options

There are two main approaches to securing the data: keep it in a data vault with access control in place, or use a rights management approach. A data vault is an encrypted data repository (e.g., database, document store) with the decryption keys given only to authorized personnel. This means that, if anyone needs access to the data, their request must be approved by the data custodian, who then gives them the decryption keys. Without the keys, the data is meaningless. One way to invoke a secure data repository is to use file system protection to give the appropriate access only to approved persons. Windows file shares are a form of data vault because only those users who have been granted access, often via the AD folder settings, can access the files. Yet another mechanism is to put the protected files in a document repository system on a protected subnet behind a firewall, and configure the firewall to allow access by approved personnel.

There are also multiple ways in which a rights management approach can be deployed. They rely on setting metadata on files, which controls who can access a file and what they can do with it. With information rights management (IRM), it is possible to allow someone to view a file but not allow them to edit, save, or print it.

Secure data repositories are best for secure document repositories—that is, files that contain corporate intellectual property that, if released, could cause damage to the organization.

A rights management approach is most appropriate for sharing information within a team, especially if team members work cooperatively on documents even though some are external. IRM gives the ability to invoke fine-grained, individual document rights to persons in the team.

Either option requires a robust and accurate IdM system to be in place within the company. In order to deploy a secure information-sharing solution, information such as department, job position, and AD group membership will be used to determine access to data and must therefore be accurate. It is equally important that as soon as a person leaves the company, his or her access rights are revoked. Of course, most organizations will use a mix of technologies. IRM might be used to share protected files within a department, while a secure data repository is used for corporate documents (e.g., board meeting minutes, financial information, audit reports).

Secure Data Repository

Establishing and maintaining a secure data repository is not a trivial exercise. The facility needs to support encryption, which means managing keys, and it requires the establishment of rules for access control. The key management requirement will vary depending on the type of keys being utilized. The simplest is a synchronous key operation in which the same keys are used for both ends of the transaction. Asynchronous keys are more secure, but policy on key validity must be addressed. A full public key infrastructure (PKI) deployment will require the establishment of a certificate authority (CA), hardware security modules, and revocation lists. For documents that must be stored in perpetuity, expiring certificates are a source of concern because a method to access to a document that has been signed by a key from an expired certificate needs to be accommodated. If there is no need for external access to a secure data repository, a simple configuration is to use a protected subnet and place the document repository behind the firewall. Maintaining access control within the firewall configuration then simplifies the task of keeping documents secure.

Rights Management

Rights management enables "seamless" protection of documents and files from the time they are created to the time they are destroyed, regardless of where the document is stored and to whom it is sent. A properly encoded document can be sent outside the company's network, and the document will still carry the restrictions imposed at document creation.

Rights management is designed for unstructured data. It is not meaningful for databases, and indeed, database technology has strong and highly granular functionality for data sharing.

It is necessary, however, to have applications that are "rights aware." Microsoft has been a leader in deploying rights management, and all Microsoft Office products are rights aware. The Microsoft Azure environment takes rights management to new heights. Azure Rights Management (RMS) enables wide collaboration within the Windows environment.

One of the issues with RMS is the granularity with which documents are to be classified. It is important that companies that engage IRM technology properly plan their classification scheme and ensure that all users adhere to the scheme. Automated, policy-based tools can be employed. There are particularly useful for classifying legacy documents, but such content-inspection functionality can also be used to "suggest" classification to users at the time of document creation.

The Secure Data vs. Rights Management Continuum

A useful approach to determining a preferred secure information-sharing approach is to map corporate requirements to a continuum, as shown in Figure 9.1, with secure data repositories at one end and rights management solutions at the other.

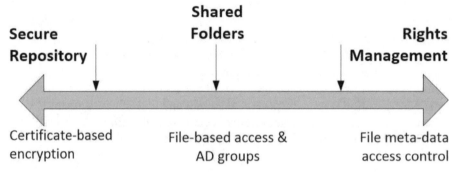

Figure 9.1: The secure data vs. rights management continuum

If the requirement is to keep board-level documents safe, a secure repository approach would be quite adequate, where each board member has been given a certificate for encryption. This will allow them to decrypt the documents they need to access for board meeting purposes, and to encrypt documents for other board members. A certificate approach will normally require digital certificates to be held in the user's identity repository record for access by the authentication system that protects the secure repository.

Note: Using network protection—putting the server for board meetings behind a firewall and establishing an AD group for board members—will protect their documents at rest but not once they have left the server. Encryption will ensure that only those users with the appropriate decryption key will be able to read the documents.

At the other end of the continuum is the rights management approach, in which individuals who create documents can classify them and select who can explicitly access them, and if they can access them, the permissions they have for editing, printing, or saving the document. Such systems will need access to the organization's identity repository to verify a user's credentials in order to determine their permissions to access the protected resource. Increasingly, such rights management systems are being combined with a classification mechanism that will mark a document as secret, confidential, or personal and will, via policies established for the business, ensure that the conditions of access and user attributes satisfy the policy when access to a particular document is requested. (This will be discussed in more detail in the Classification section, page 175.)

Between these two extremes are file system functions that allow access by multiple users to designated folders. Shared folders in a Windows environment typically grant access to the documents and subfolders in the share to enrolled groups. This approach provides users access to resources typically on a group basis—that is, if you are in the appropriate AD group, you will get access to a shared folder and any file in the folder or subfolder. Access can be granted at varying levels as permitted under the file system: create, read, update, and delete.

Data Loss Prevention

The astute reader will have noted that secure data sharing is actually part of an organization's approach to data loss prevention (DLP). Unfortunately, the term DLP has been hijacked by networking types and typically refers to network edge devices that monitor data leaving an organization's network and stop any file or document that contains data deemed to be sensitive. Content filtering is an increasingly popular technology whereby real-time monitoring of data leaving the network seeks to identify potential exfiltration of protected information. API gateways seek to manage the network edge by controlling the communication to controlled files. This means that users will be required to authenticate via the gateway before gaining access to protected information. Figure 9.2 shows the technologies that comprise DLP.

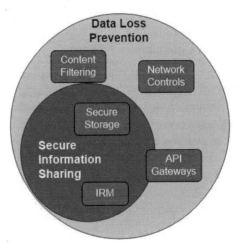

Figure 9.2: Data loss prevention

For instance, if a policy is established that any file containing a credit card number is embargoed and must not be sent outside the company network, DLP infrastructure will stop any documents with identifiable credit card detail. While this is commendable, and there are bona fide reasons for DLP installations to block such detail, there are a few problems. What if the file is being sent to your acquiring bank to process a transaction? The file will be stopped. Hopefully a notification will be generated, but then a manual process will need to be invoked to release the file.

Or what if a policy is established that prohibits documents on a sensitive project to be sent outside the company? Team members who want to send a file to an external lawyer for a legal review will have to manually intervene, or find another way to get the file to the lawyer. File encryption is also a problem. If a sensitive file is encrypted, the network device, which depends on content inspection, will not be able to detect that sensitive information is potentially leaving the organization.

Other DLP methods for securing data include firewalls and other network-level devices, and API gateways that can provide very sophisticated communication controls, even to the point of supporting policies that determine the attributes of users with specific access entitlements.

Strategic Approach

As with most pieces of the IT puzzle, a strategic approach is recommended. This will avoid the deployment of point solutions that, while solving one pain point, do not neatly fit under the IT strategic management umbrella. Deployment of secure sharing technology should be part of an organization's DLP solution, which in turn is part of the IT governance framework.

Another component of the strategy is a change management program to develop a security culture within the organization. Security necessarily limits access to files and documents. Although, in a perfect world no one should need to access a document to which they have been denied access, in reality it will be necessary for staff to request access to a protected document from time to time. When this happens, it should be in the full knowledge that this is to be expected and should not be accompanied by a resentful comment about "those guys in IT." In fact, invoking a document/file classification mechanism to heighten staff appreciation for information protection is generally a good idea.

Principles

In developing secure information sharing, it is important that a governance approach is adopted to ensure consistency across the organization, or at least across business units within the organization.

- Under the "least rights" principle, staff are only given access to the least amount of sensitive documentation that is required for them to perform their jobs. Many organizations don't do this. For example, when a new staff member joins the organization, they are given access to the same systems and file shares as someone else in their work unit. If that person has at some time been given elevated privileges, which were not revoked, the new staff member will receive the same elevated privileges. Identity management systems these days all include approval workflows. Staff should be provisioned independently, and access rights should be approved appropriately for each new staff member.

- A classification approach should be mandated that will either allow users the freedom to classify their own documents or force machine classification. In the former, the system can "suggest" a classification based on content inspection for keywords in the document or file, or it can automatically classify. Some form of machine classification is typically required at commencement of the deployment of a secure information-sharing environment because existing documents will need to be classified.

A Data-Centric Approach

A useful methodology when selecting a secure data sharing solution is to consider the requirements of the company as data is used within the organization.

Data at Rest

Protecting data at rest is most appropriate for organizations that have repositories of protected information, such as documents pertaining to the company's intellectual property (e.g., product development plan and business strategy documents). These files will typically be encrypted, so management of keys will be important. Such protected repositories will often sit behind network firewalls; if this is the case, access through the firewall should be based on a user's identity attributes. Users with access rights should have the decryption keys to allow them to read the documents. The cloud has complicated this scenario with the need to secure data at rest even if it is stored in the cloud repository. The identity store is critical for these access control requirements since an identity provider service will typically supply a SAML assertion to guide the cloud-based access control decision (see chapter 4 for more information).

Data in Motion

A secure data repository is not much use if the data is decrypted and then transmitted in clear text between the server and the client device. A comprehensive secure information-sharing environment will ensure that an appropriate method of secure communication is in place. This might be as simple as using an SSL connection for HTTP sessions, or it might be as complex as deploying virtual private networks (VPNs) for any external access to sensitive data.

The classic solution is to use SSL, which means the use of encryption keys (which need to be managed) for the sender who encrypts the message and the receiver who decrypts the message.

Other solutions include the use of rights management, in which case there may be no need to encrypt files because IRM will provide the necessary protection, or encrypted files from the data repository, again obviating the need for SSL. If a file is only decrypted by keys on the user's PC, there's no need for SSL because the transmitted file will already be encrypted.

Data in Use

Analysis of how application data is used by endpoint clients will identify situations in which the organization is being unnecessary exposed to risk. There are basically two ways to manage control over files in use: IRM can be used, which will control what a user can do with the file to which they are provided access, or a special client can be used that manages the permissions of document recipients. If the receiver is given read-only rights to a document, that's all they will be able to do with it. If access to applications is coming from mobile devices, external to the organization, organizations should be concerned that sensitive data is being displayed in situations that might compromise security. A possible solution is to deploy a risk management score when granting access to a protected resource. Access from an external mobile device outside of business hours would be scored differently from an access request from within a corporate network during business hours.

For access by a mobile device, there are a number of ways to improve the security level of access to corporate resources. Developing a native app that can incorporate an authentication mechanism such as OpenID connect with OAuth tokens can positively identify the device or user. Two-factor authentication, using the device as "something they have," can readily be implemented, too.

Classification

Secure information sharing requires a classification mechanism, which is the process of marking a document based on its conformance to a set of characteristics determined for a group of documents.

When it comes to a classification process, there are some defined steps to go through:

1. Determine how protective markings should be applied. This can be done either automatically, via a set of policies that are applied to a document when it's created, or it can be left up to the user who is responsible for classifying a document when they create it and save it for the first time. The system can prompt the user based on content inspection of the document.

2. Decide when protective markings should be applied. Most classification systems apply markings upon creation of a document. In some cases, this occurs as the document leaves the company's network.

3. Determine the process for updating a document's markings. It is usual to have a function within a business that oversees document classifications and has the authority to change them. An administrative center that has governance over data loss protection will be able to alter a classification if it does not adhere to policy. An automated routine that continually checks document repositories will identify documents for potential re-classification.

4. Define duration of classifications. The length of time during which a document's classification is active must be determined. This will vary depending on the sensitivity of the document. Statutory periods for document retention, archive policy, business continuity plans, and community relations will also impact classification duration.

These elements of a company's document classification policy should be documented in the organization's policy statement regarding protection of corporate intellectual property and the organization's response to regulatory controls, including privacy.

There is an international standard for classification schemes. ISO 27001 recommends that a four-step process, shown in Figure 9.3, be defined to ensure that a comprehensive solution is put in place.

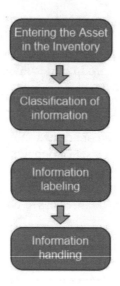

Figure 9.3: Information classification process

The first step is to inventory the document and file assets. This will ensure 1) all assets will be included in the inventory of documents to be protected and 2) the classification scheme will be comprehensive—that is, covering all such documents and not just pertinent to a few.

The second step is to classify the information. Each document will be categorized in accordance with its classification.

The third step is to place markings on each document or file. This will require an appropriate software product. For Office documents, the built-in rights management capability can be utilized. If a software tool is acquired, it can be used to apply the metadata markings.

The fourth step is to enforce the correct handling of documents and files in accordance with their markings. It might be necessary for users to download client software for their various devices to enable the classification markings to be observed.

ISO 27001 also recommends that the selected classification scheme encompass all document formats. Table 9.1 shows the classification scheme for documents, with the procedures for each format of the three controlled information types.

Table 9.1: Classification scheme

	Internal	**Restricted**	**Secret**
Electronic documents	Restrictions on detachable storage	Automated watermarking of documents	Access control only available to approved persons
Information systems	Internal documents available only to persons with a "staff" designation	Documents available only to persons with a "Restricted" classification	Documents available only to persons with a "Secret" AD group
Paper documents	Documents must be appropriately stored when not being referenced	Documents must be maintained in secure files	Document checkout processes to be followed
Storage media	Can be stored in public repositories if protected via RMS	Storage limited to data center infrastructure	Documents may be stored only in the appropriate encrypted file store
Verbal information	Staff to be aware of the protected nature of information	Staff cautioned to observe protection processes (e.g., not discuss in public areas)	Discussion only in protected areas
Email	Unrestricted email internally, embargoed pending investigation for external mail recipients	To be shared only with appropriately classified personnel	To be shared only between members of the Secret group

In this circumstance, a three-level classification scheme has been selected: Internal documents (i.e., not for transmittal outside the company), Restricted documents (i.e., distribution limited to specified groups), and Confidential documents (i.e., documents available to specific persons). There is, of course, another category: unrestricted, for documents that are not controlled.

Now a word about deploying a classification system. At one end of the continuum is a mechanistic approach whereby automated decisions on document classification are made, and punitive consequences are applied. At the other end is a cognitive approach whereby humans make the access decision, and their reward/recognition system is implemented.

As with any project such as this, the main challenge is to instill an awareness of security within the organization. To do this, it is recommended that a change management initiative be initiated. Staff need to be educated about the need to maintain security at the system level, protecting login accounts; at the document level, accurately marking documents; and at the physical level, not leaving sensitive documents on an unoccupied desk.

Change management does require high-level involvement—ideally at board level to ensure policy is accurately set and communicated. This will also illustrate any changes that might be required with the identity and access management environment. If the IdM environment can't support the requirements of the classification scheme, an upgrade project must be undertaken to develop the required functionality.

Generally speaking, to make cultural change within an organization, a "carrot" rather than a "stick" approach is preferable. This means using reward/recognition rather than punishment. Securing information is an ideal situation in which a competitive approach can be employed, with departments or workgroups being recognized for deploying programs that work and staff are engaged staff in the data protection task.

Public Key Infrastructure

One technology that has a place in some secure information sharing environments is PKI. PKI is a mechanism to add a layer of security to a user's activity that makes it virtually impossible to circumvent, provided the mechanism for creating and distributing keys is strong enough. A PKI validation of a user's identity can be trusted to a very high level. Man-in-the-middle attacks are not possible, and communication is secure.

Figure 9.4 depicts the major components of a PKI environment.

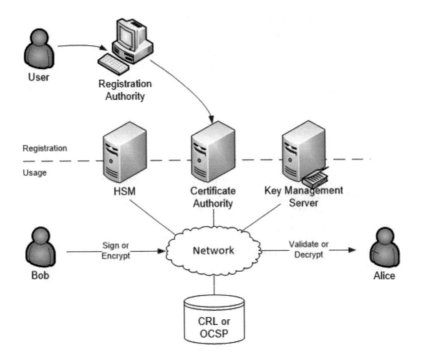

Figure 9.4: PKI environment

Participants must first be enrolled in the scheme. The registration authority (RA) validates an applicant's credentials and requests the generation of a certificate from the CA. The CA generates a key pair, or requests their generation from a Hardware Security Module (HSM), and creates a certificate. It writes the public key to a repository such as a certificate store and/or key management service and provides the private key to the user via a secure method. In a secure information-sharing environment, there will likely be a need to manage keys, including expired keys, for document decryption purposes.

Note: Classic PKI uses a certificate revocation list (CRL) of all compromised certificates that can be checked at any time. If a certificate is not in the CRL, it's deemed to be valid (provided its expiry date has not been reached). A variant of the PKI standard allows for a certificate server to be made available via the OCSP protocol, which provides a positive assurance of a certificate's validity.

The operation of a PKI environment is quite simple, and consists of two "actions":

- Registration—Users register their participation in the PKI by accessing the RA, completing the necessary identity validation process, and requesting a certificate. The RA will then contact the CA, which will generate a key pair, usually via the HSM. The CA will then send the public key to the key management or certificate server and the private key to the user via a hardware token such as a smart card, or by emailing a link to a secure API to download the key to the private key store of the user's system.

- Usage—There are two use cases:
    - o User digitally signs a document—The signing system uses the user's private key to create a piece of code that's attached to the document. When the recipient wants to verify the signature, they access the user's public key to verify the signature.
    - o User encrypts a document—The encrypting system uses the recipient's public key and creates a hash of the document. The recipient then uses their private key to decrypt the document.

The RA process has a direct bearing on the strength of the PKI. The RA's process of verifying identities of applicants must be "vetted" to ensure it meets the required level of identity assurance. The methodology of generating keys and the way in which private keys are provided to users combine to indicate the robustness of the PKI. A very strong key-generation process can be compromised if private keys can be intercepted during their transmittal to the applicant.

The CA process must also be evaluated to ensure that the generation of keys is robust and that the management of the key store is appropriate. For instance, if a CRL is being used, the frequency of update must match the requirement for the PKI environment. In some cases, CRLs are updated as soon as a compromised certificate is identified—for example, when a staff member leaves the company's employ. Sometimes the CRLs are updated nightly, but in other cases, CRL updates are only performed weekly. Given that a requirement of most PKIs is that the CRL or OCSP server should be contacted whenever a transaction is undertaken, the frequency of CRL or OCSP update must be fit-for-purpose.

Key management is another important consideration for a PKI deployment. Only trusted individuals should have access to the encryption keys, be they PKI certificate keys, database encryption keys, or even SSL session keys. Key management is an important activity and should require a four-eyes process for any key creation or rotation task.

The use of an HSM to secure keys and the use of corporately generated keys, rather than vendor-supplied keys, should be considered. For a PKI establishment, a "key ceremony" should be undertaken whereby key managers are commissioned.

A related issue is the selection of the CA. At one end of the spectrum are highly secure CAs, typically military, with robust registration processes. At the other end are self-signed certificates that use exactly the same technology, but the level of security provided depends upon the RA procedures and the certificate generation process. One consideration is the selection of a root CA. If a seamless enrollment process is required, a public CA supported under the Windows environment will be required, but this will require the purchase of certificates. If self-signed certificates are used, this cost is eliminated, but users will need to import the company's certificate into their browsers.

Benefits

It's worthwhile reflecting on the benefits of deploying a well-thought-out, secure information-sharing environment. There are at least four benefits that should be balanced against the cost of deploying a solution. Part of the strategy planning should include a risk management exercise to evaluate their "expected values":

- Reduced litigation costs—In the event of a security breach, there will likely be related, and probably expensive, litigation. It's far better to avoid the breach in the first place.

- Reduced reputational-damage costs—Increasingly, as organizations know more about their customers, the need to protect this information increases. While members of the public will entrust organizations with their details, some quite sensitive, they equally expect that it will be adequately protected. The reputational damage that a compromise might cause is significant and potentially disastrous.

- Reduced administration costs—The cost of administering corporate security is significant and, more often than not, inadequately captured. When a policy violation is identified, it is expensive to investigate the violation manually. Tools to reduce false positives represent a cost reduction, and management processes that automate investigations have short payback time frames.

- Better cultural awareness—The development of a security culture within an organization is fraught with difficulty. It can easily go off the rails and cause frustration within the organization when staff experience constraints on their ability to do things with documents. For example, if someone who used to be able to send documents to an external business partner is now prevented from doing so, they need to appreciate why.

Conclusion

Secure information sharing is a seminal activity for organizations. Sharing information securely enables business to be conducted while protecting intellectual property and commercial-in-confidence information. Organizations should take a strategic approach to designing, commissioning, and operating their IT environments to provide the requisite protection.

A company's identity and access management (IAM) environment must support secure information sharing by providing the necessary information to determine whether a requesting user has the necessary entitlements for access; this will allow the system to determine their specific rights to the requested resource. For a secure repository solution, this means providing access to the user ID of the requesting user so that it can be checked against the access control list. For a rights management sharing system, the IdP will typically need to provide more detail, such as the user's department or workgroup membership, to allow a determination of the access rights they should be granted. For AD group-based systems, the IAM must ensure that the UID of the user is in the appropriate group. For certificate-based systems, this means that the certificate should be available from the data store.

Use Case: PharmaCo

Scenario	PharmaCo is a pharmaceutical company that develops medicine for human consumption and application. The company has an active research and development group that is continually bringing new products to the marketplace.
	PharmaCo works with a large number of researchers employed at several different universities and research establishments nationally and internationally. Legal representation is external to the company, as is their marketing/advertising agency.
	PharmaCo is conducting clinical trials on a new drug to inhibit the progress of type 2 diabetes. It uses new university research that shows promise in the animal trials that have just been completed.
Strategy	In light of recent incidents of loss-of-IP at some of its competitors, PharmaCo has decided to institute a data-loss prevention environment that will reduce the likelihood of loss of sensitive documents, such as research findings, marketing campaign details, contract documents, and business plans.
Solution	A rights management system was selected for the product development. It was determined that the file store would be on a public cloud service that

would allow project team members to share documents with external project team members. This requires all external team members to be provisioned into the corporate identity access environment and added to the appropriate AD groups. A self-service tool will be deployed on the corporate website for authorized users to request changes to their access rights.

A classification tool is also required that continually monitors documents and file stores. An assisted classification scheme has been selected whereby the tool recommends a classification category for newly created or modified documents. An email solution that ensures restrictions are placed on email sent within, and external to, the project team is part of the solution.

A data-loss protection product that monitors for unusual behavior, such as out-of-pattern document access, out-of-hours access, and abnormal quantity access, is also part of the solution. In some cases, it will be configured to embargo a document activity pending review by a security authority; in some cases, it will issue a notification for analysis.

In addition, a secure project repository for project archives is included. Cloud storage is to be used for the document store, and enrollment in the appropriate AD group is required to obtain access to the archive file share.

Q & A

Q. With the accelerating rate of change occurring in technology (e.g., cloud service, BYOD, IoT), is it not inevitable that data loss will occur and that only cursory protection therefore needs to be provided?

A. No. Although the task of protecting data is becoming more complex, solutions are becoming increasingly more powerful. An important aspect of security is to not reach a state of inevitability that precludes a well-thought-out strategy from being developed. A strategic approach will accommodate the risks that are important to mitigate and will identify those issues that are going to happen. Only then is it possible to craft a secure information-sharing approach that is optimized for the specific situation in which an organization operates.

To deploy a DLP network edge device without considering the organization's full requirements, or deploying a rights management solution without a change management initiative to modify the security culture within the company, should be avoided.

Q. PKI is often discounted because it is too costly and is considered "overkill" for most companies. Is there any point in considering PKI for an information security application?

A. While many organizations have decided against deploying PKI for cost reasons, that is no reason to discount its use. Anecdotal evidence suggests that in some cases, PKI deployments do not proceed because of adverse advice from legal counsel that fails to take a risk-management approach to deployment options. Such advice only considers high-security, and therefore costly, deployment options rather than accepting a solution that is eminently satisfactory for an organization.

On the IT side, the complexity and cost of key management has been known to "kill" a PKI deployment. Rather than craft a solution to accommodate the specific requirements of the business, IT managers have been known to put key management in the "too hard" basket, thereby losing the benefit of a mature and effective technology.

PKI is a bona fide technology and well suits the document security task. It provides a level of user management that other technologies cannot approach. It should be included in the list of technologies to be considered when forming a secure information-sharing strategy.

Q. Our network operations staff have selected an edge DLP device that monitors documents leaving the organization's network. Isn't this sufficient?

A. Maybe. It's hard to know until a strategic review of the organization's requirement has been conducted and the options evaluated. A DLP device at an exfiltration point can be very beneficial in identifying documents and files being sent externally to the company's network. These devices employ content filtering looking for matches to keywords and templates that suggest a specific classification level. For instance, if "Project Hyperion" has been deemed "restricted," when a document with the word "Hyperion" is identified by the DLP device in a file transfer or as an email attachment, the device can either let the action finish but send a notification to security, quarantine the document until it is manually investigated and either permitted or denied, or embargo the document and prohibit the transfer.

The main issue is the manual effort, and associated cost, of managing such an environment. If a rights management system is employed, such DLP devices become less of a benefit, and costs might be reduced by de-commissioning the device or only using it to flag those abuses that are considered major.

Chapter 10

Consumerization

I remember an interview I had with an IT consultant some time ago. He was frustrated that the IT Forum, of which we were members, did not share his passion for the retail sector and the immense benefits IT analytics could afford the myriad small-to-medium enterprises (SMEs) who dealt with the public on a daily basis. We were sitting in a coffee shop in a large shopping mall, and to illustrate his point, we left our table and went to the nearest retail establishment, which happened to be a women's dress shop. The lady at the cash register turned out to be the store manager, and he asked her what difference it would make if she knew more about her customers, their buying preferences, and propensity to purchase. "I would double my profit," was her response. In asking why, it turned out that maintaining her gross margin depended on selling what she called "first flight" product—product that sells before it hits the discount cycle. By knowing her customer's preferences earlier (i.e., before the inventory analysis report), she could get more of what customers wanted onto the racks and move it before the stale stock controls cut in. I was suitably impressed.

As technology has progressed, consumerization has become easier and exponentially more important. Digital transformation will literally put a significant segment of the SME market out of business and propel a significant number of SMEs to new levels of prosperity. Consumerization will be increasingly important and the focus of a large amount of time and money over the next few years. Unfortunately, some companies will not be able to adapt and will become digital transformation victims. But there will be at least as many companies that will adapt to the new consumerization offerings, and they will enjoy new heights of profitability.

CIDM Trajectory

So where are we coming from and where are we going with customer/citizen identity management (CIDM)? We'll use the term "consumer" as encompassing both customers of commercial organizations and citizens of government organizations.

There is little doubt that consumer service is undergoing systemic and immense change. We can only speculate where this is going. As the cost of big data analysis continues to drop and technology with which consumers can be engaged becomes more prevalent, more and more commercial organizations will reach out to promote their services and manage consumer interaction.

We are currently observing a convergence of identity management (IdM) and customer relationship management (CRM), as shown in Figure 10.1.

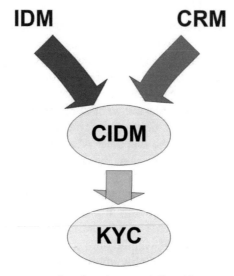

Figure 10.1: Identity management and customer relationship management convergence

Organizations with a CRM system that has served them well as a call center tool to keep track of customer interaction now want to extend the system to record transactions so that an analysis can be performed and custom promotion can be employed. That means that we need an IdM tool that will allow us to identify consumers as they purchase our products and services, so that we can understand buyer behavior and propensity to purchase. The end result is a "know-your-customer" capability that lets us not only satisfy their requirements but also meet their experiential expectations. Whereas the baby boomer generation is focused on value, and buying at a low price, millennials are focused on user experience, and will walk if they don't get it.

Baby boomers	Focused on value—this demographic defines its worth from their work. They have worked hard to build their prosperity and appreciate job security. They want high quality and low prices.
Millennials	Focused on experience—they are ambitious and multi-tasking, and appreciate flex-time and sabbaticals. They are not motivated primarily by low cost and will gladly pay more for a good experience. They will switch suppliers readily in response to good or bad reviews of customer experience.

Understanding our target market means that we need to electronically know our customer better. We need to know their purchase habits and be able to predict their propensity to purchase our products and services.

Know Your Customer

In terms of identity management to support consumerization, the identity data solution is quite shallow but very wide. For instance, within the financial sector there is no hierarchical requirement with inherited attributes down a deep tree, which can occur on the staff identity side, but there is a requirement to be able to join a customer's identity across banking, wealth creation, insurance, and the other products that banks provide. Relationship management is paramount: the need to know and manage a customer's relationships with the bank as well as external service providers such as financial advisers and insurance agents.

The Early Years

Know your customer (KYC) started as an anti-money laundering (AML) initiative in the financial industry. It was part of the customer due diligence processes put in place to ensure all bank accounts could be traced back to the entities that owned them, thereby making it much more difficult for a business to be set up for the express purpose of receiving money from illegal activity and repurposing it as revenue from legitimate commercial activity.

One of the issues with many banks' KYC initiatives has been their focus on AML regulation rather than on the significant benefits that a properly constituted program can afford. Banks have typically considered KYC as a non-core competence with significant cost for training and audit purposes. In some cases, KYC has led to significant customer dissatisfaction because of the demands for documentation and significant delays in the establishment of bank accounts. With customer data spread over multiple disparate systems in what is typically a very siloed environment, many banks have been unable to engage in the deep data analytics, across all their data stores, that can afford them competitive advantage.

In fact, KYC can be considered as a continuum (Figure 10.2), with business protection at one end and business enablement at the other. Both are important; there's not much point in developing business enablement factors such as consumer IdM and improved relationship management if factors such as data-loss protection and real-time security intelligence are not also considered.

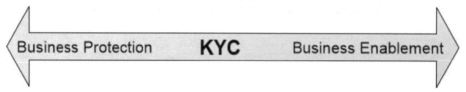

Figure 10.2: KYC continuum

Where We're Going

Gone are the days of interactive voice recorders to ensure that your customers don't talk to a human being. No longer should websites be devoid of contact phone numbers or email addresses to make it difficult for your customers to contact you. Systems to facilitate customer feedback are required in order to understand the difficulties customers have with our products/services. We want to hear from sales staff what our customers are asking for.

KYC has gone mainstream. Understanding what customers want and meeting or exceeding their expectations is part of running a successful business. As baby boomers, with a focus on value, give way to millennials, with a focus on experience, knowing your customer becomes increasingly important. This means combining the data you know about them—demographics, relationships, and buying habits—into a picture that will let you gauge their propensity to purchase so that you can engage in targeted promotion. CRMs have evolved from recording devices to predictive tools that have the potential to significantly improve business profitability.

> Recently I wanted to purchase some DIY wood flooring at a box hardware store. The room where it was to be installed required the flooring to have a certain noise-dampening level. The salesperson told me the noise-attenuating flooring had not been rated, so it was not suitable. I asked if he would pass that requirement on to the manufacturer. "They don't ask us for customer feedback" was his response!

The Customer Experience

Providing a good customer experience has never been more important than it is today. The baby boomer generation, who lived through the transition from personal service at the grocery store to queuing for the privilege of paying at supermarkets, is giving way to generation X and millennials who are less concerned with getting a low price, but more concerned with enjoying a good experience. They want a coffee with their haircut and will pay for the privilege.

Websites

Company websites are typically quite poor and attract much criticism. This is a concern if the target market is millennials who, rather than complain, switch. The websites of most large organizations grow as new services are added with little thought to the effect on customer service. The result is a site on which services take too long to find and are too hard to understand.

> A recent service requirement on a government website was so poorly described that it was necessary to travel to a customer service center and have the service levels explained in person. Not only did this cost the citizen in time and money, it required the government agency to provide a service desk with knowledgeable staff. Both could have been avoided with a little forethought and a better-designed website.

All website changes should be subjected to a focus group activity to evaluate the impact they have on the rest of the site and to ensure that customer expectations are being met.

Another aspect of providing customers with a good online experience is to ensure they can easily use their smartphones to access the corporate website. This means that websites must be responsive—resizing for small screens, and not require passwords to be entered.

KYC requires identification of website visitors, which means that the IdM system must accommodate the level of assurance needed for the service being consumed. This will normally be a level 1 assurance (see chapter 4) that can be accommodated via a social login such as GoogleID, Facebook, or Microsoft Live, which will identify the user but not require them to set up an account or remember additional passwords. The technology is available to do this; it just needs to be deployed.

Mobile Strategy

The use of mobile devices continues to increase. There is no doubt that consumers want to connect via mobile devices, be it something they hold such as a smartphone or something they wear such as a watch or clothing sensor. Consumers expect devices to be supported, and, if we want a meaningful dialog with them, it is necessary to support such connections. In fact, those businesses that do will enjoy a richer and more profitable experience.

This means that we must support standards. OpenID Connect is the preferred connection standard for mobile devices. It can be augmented with OAuth tokens for greater authentication assurance or Fast ID On-line (FIDO) for higher levels of assurance.

IoT

"Things" with which consumers can interact are getting cheaper and easier to work with (see chapter 7). Organizations that can facilitate this—for example, by making their Fitbit data more easy to understand and share, making their cars communicate with the service center, or providing control to their house devices, will do well. There are two major aspects of providing such a service. First, it must be intuitively easy, as users will not tolerate having to learn a complex process. Second, it must be secure; it is expected that regulatory controls with be observed and that sensitive information will be protected.

There is little doubt that IoT and consumerization are the two trends that will dominate societal change over the next few years. Innovative solutions that effectively join developments in these areas represent significant potential for agile companies to offer profitable products and services to the marketplace.

Customer IdM

A crucial problem for anyone extending online services to members of the public is how to identify them. For employees and contractors, we build identity management and access control systems to accommodate them, but for members of the public this is simply not possible: we need other options.

There are already several options available to us, and more will develop over the next few years. One option is to use a public IdP, an organization providing online services to which users subscribe. Public IdPs collect basic detail about users who register on their site when setting up an account. These organizations then provide access to this repository for others to use for login purposes. Companies or governments that provide services to the public then have the option of inviting visitors to their website to log in using their public IdP account rather than entering usernames and passwords.

Virtually any person seeking to access an online service will have at least one public IdP account. The most popular include:

- Facebook
- Twitter
- Google
- Microsoft
- LinkedIn
- Yahoo
- PayPal
- AWS
- Salesforce
- WordPress

Using a public provider service makes a lot of sense:

- It's not necessary to establish an identity store with the attendant cost and liability. To establish a service large enough for all potential customers could be a significant undertaking.
- Customers don't like entering their details into websites unless they absolutely must do so.
- Customers will often be using small devices such as a smartphone and will prefer being able to connect using a social login account.

The biggest issue is, is the public IdP's registration process sufficient to positively identify people to a satisfactory level for the transaction being undertaken? Typically, all a user of a public IdP needs to do is to provide a valid email address. There is no validation of their name, address, date of birth, or other credentials.

For organizations that want to allow customers to undertake a transaction, such a low level of authentication may not be sufficient. A "level of assessment" analysis is recommended (see chapter 4 for more detail).

> An Australian university needed to promote courses of interest and encourage enrollments. It was decided to allow visitors to register their interest via the use of public IdPs to capture email address for promotional purposes.
>
> But this account was not sufficient for an enrolled student. New students were required to show a photo ID in order to establish an account on the university's student portal.

Higher-level Identity Provider Services

It is clear that in many cases a higher-order authentication service is required; the question is, who will provide it and on what basis? There are several organizations that collect and store identity data about their clients; a natural extension of their business model would be to offer identity provider services.

Banks

With the development of AML regulation, establishing a bank account is an increasingly demanding experience. It is necessary to verify your identity to a high degree. Typically, a 100-point check is required that will involve verifying identity-breeder documents, such as birth certificate and marriage certificate, as well as a photo identity document, such as a passport or driver license. A bank-validated identity, therefore, has a high level of confidence associated with it.

Banks are also usually regarded as trustworthy. Most people will provide identity information to their bank and trust that it will be kept secure. This means that banks are in an ideal position to act as an identity provider service with customers controlling what information they want to release, when it can be released, and to whom.

Telcos

Telephone companies are also ideal candidates to act as an identity provider because they have typically authenticated customers to a high level. They know where we live, our phone number, and often our Internet service details. They also have a built-in payment process whereby they can charge for acting in this capacity.

Government

Another potential source of identity provision is government. Although acting as an identity provider is not a core competence for government because their mandate is to provide government services, the government does have a highly regarded repository of identity information and could provide a direct IdP service, or anchor a commercial service, for the benefit of companies that need to identify members of the public.

It is important to acknowledge a polarization in most geographies between those who trust government and have no qualms about providing identity information to the government, and those who want to disclose as little information as possible to government agencies. While governments acting as a IdP for citizens makes sense from technical viewpoint, it is likely that there will be significant resistance in certain quarters.

Life Management Platforms

There is an increasing trend for members of the public to be able to control their identity data and release it on an as required, need-to-know basis. That is, consumers will manage the identity data that is provided as they navigate online services. A life management platform (LMP) does this effectively; users enter the data they want to store, and then release information if and when it's needed. The advantage of using an LMP is the ability to have one location act as the source of truth for a person's identity regardless of whether it's a personal application, a work application, or a commercial application. Since LMPs offer a generic identity store, the LMP can typically be configured by users to release context-appropriate identity data depending upon the service being engaged. Popular pure-play LMPs are organizations such as Only Once and Meeco.

Citizen IdM: What's Government Doing?

Most governments have realized that they must emphasize online channels and go digital. It's too expensive to maintain call center or service center channels for the delivery of government services. Many governments now have a "digital first" policy that requires government departments to make services available on the Internet first, whenever possible.

This matches what most citizens want, too. Standing in a line at a government office to access a service is close to the bottom of the list of fun things to do. If at all possible, we want to renew our driver's license or pay our taxes online, at a time convenient for us. That frees us up to do more enjoyable or profitable activities during the daytime.

But how does a government department authenticate users? How do they identify an online user to connect them to the appropriate service with a high level of assurance that the right person is connected to the right record?

There are basically two approaches that governments are taking: third-party verified or a persistent ID approach.

Third-Party Verified

The third-party approach means that government does not need to store any identity information on citizens for authentication purposes. There is no central data store being maintained by government that could get compromised and cause damage or embarrassment. All data for authentication purposes is stored by a number of commercial identity provider service organizations, endorsed by government, but selected by citizens when they enroll in order to access government services.

The advantages are obvious: there is no liability on the government's part, there are no privacy issues to be concerned with, and the risk profile is quite low.

The downside is that third-party providers must be regulated in some way. There is a need to set the guidelines and initiate a conformance testing program to ensure that service providers are meeting the guidelines. The supplier might also need to be reimbursed for providing the service in situations where there would be a net cost to the company because usage of the service is too low. Or the vendor may need to be subsidized for a period of time.

The UK, with the GOV.UK Verify service, is an example of a government that uses a third-party approach.

Persistent ID

Some governments are setting up their own identity repositories and requiring citizens to establish an account in order to access government services. In this scenario, users establish an account at an assurance level commensurate with the government services they wish to consume.

The advantage of this approach is the ability of government to manage the level of registration it requires in order to grant access to a service. To pay a vehicle annual road tax fee, a relatively low level of authentication (level 1) is satisfactory. To access a driver demerit point record, a higher level of authentication (level 2) will generally be required because it's more important that this information is not inadvertently released. Maintaining an identity store enables government to better control the level to which a user's identity has been verified.

It also allows government to better manage a citizen's session with departments. For instance, in the case above, the service could pass the user's driver license detail to the department of motor vehicles so that they can connect the session to correct the record within the department's database.

The disadvantage is the cost of providing the service and the liability the government takes on by storing citizen identity data. If this repository is compromised, there could be significant embarrassment for the government. For this reason, governments should not store any more information than is absolutely necessary in the citizen identity store.

Many continental European countries follow a persistent ID methodology, as does New Zealand with the RealMe service, Singapore, Hong Kong, and Australia.

Market Sector Responses

The way in which organizations respond to the market as consumerization takes hold will be a defining moment for business success. Consumerization will impact virtually all commercial and public sector organizations.

Four industry sectors are exemplars of the issues that must be addressed by virtually all industry sectors:

Financial

As noted previously, the financial industry must move beyond KYC for just regulatory purposes and exploit technology to provide extended services for customers. Banks have been recalcitrant in providing good customer service; they have systematically reduced face-to-face services for customers. They have closed branches, closed business units for all but high net worth individuals, moved customers to ATMs, and removed contact details from websites. This is perplexing since banking is one area in which customer service is paramount. A banking startup that can provide customer service more effectively and more efficiently by building a KYC capability is a distinct threat to the established banks.

In the 1980s at the height of diversification in the US telecom industry, a startup bragged that it had poached a high percentage of customers from a large established telecom supplier.

The established telecom company then went back through its business records to identify the high-profit customers. The company then made a very attractive offer to these customers to entice them to switch back—with a high success rate.

Another concern for banks is their disparate data stores. A bank client can have multiple data records with one in Accounts, another one in Mortgages, a third in Wealth Management, and possibly another in the Insurance department. This make it difficult to form a single view of a customer and use the information to inform decisions on whether or not to advance funds or advice. It also hampers the exploitation of the benefits that new technology can afford.

One emerging technology area of importance to a bank's KYC initiatives is artificial intelligence (AI). AI can allow banks to replace the human interface but still provide the services customers want. For instance, with sufficient KYC information, the decision on mortgage options can be made entirely online with no manual intervention. With the appropriate systems in place, the only time a meeting should be needed is the signing of the contract, and even that can be replaced in jurisdictions that support a digital signature service.

This means there is significant potential for banks to extend their wealth creation services for their customers. First, they can accurately understand customer aspirations and risk appetite. Then, they can exploit AI to implement investment monitoring and provide better advisory services to their customers than they are currently getting from their financial advisors.

As mentioned, there is another interesting identity management perspective. The large amount of identity data that banks maintain on customers provides an opportunity for banks to monetize the asset. Banks are high on the list of potential LMP providers. Customers generally trust their banks, so they would be willing to "deposit" their identity information in an "identity vault" for release when, and to whom, a customer wants. Banks also have an ideal mechanism for charging a fee for such a service.

Health Care

Health care has a complex identity management requirement. Access to health systems must be strictly controlled with doctors, nurses, other health professionals, and administrators all requiring system access at varying levels. In addition, there is a large cohort of external service providers such as radiologists, pharmacists, equipment technicians, and emergency services personnel whose access to health systems must be facilitated but controlled. On top of that, patient access must also be managed, particularly the level of consent a patient gives to components of their electronic health record.

This complex access control environment requires a sophisticated IAM solution that can adequately provision into an identity data repository that meets the relying system requirements and potentially provisions directly into health application identity repositories, or AD groups for those applications that are "AD-aware." The larger vendors of health care applications are not at the forefront of technology development, the most prevalent interface protocol for identity information being LDAP.

Then there is the question of the extent of system access that should be granted to health professionals. In many jurisdictions, each acute care facility is somewhat independent, and doctors at one facility cannot access records at another. This is obviously not ideal. While the electronic health record initiatives will be a significant step forward, jurisdictions with multiple health care facilities should maintain an integrated patient administration facility that accommodates the need of doctors for longitudinal care information. This should include both acute care and primary care facilities. At the same time, health care facility administration should ensure that privacy legislation is being adhered to. It is not satisfactory for a patient to think their data is being protected by the electronic health care record while at the same time the patient administration system is providing access to non-involved health care professionals.

Another concern for health care facilities is maintaining security over system interfaces to ensure that systems are not compromised and that sensitive information is not released. The technology is available to achieve this; all that is required is the will to make it happen (see chapter 9 for more detail).

Health care system software is complex and provides extensive access control capabilities. It is often the case that system capabilities outstrip the ability of medical facility staff to properly implement all the system features and safeguards. Software vendors are increasingly being called upon to assist health care professionals to better manage access control to health data and to facilitate the user experience by making their systems more intuitive and simpler to administer. There's also a need for software vendors to support up-to-date protocols. For cloud-based authentication, this means supporting SAML assertions; for provisioning into an identity management environment, SCIM should be used; and externalizing decision-making to an authorization server should use XACML.

> In a health jurisdiction in Australia, the same medical software was installed in hospitals as well as clinics. In the hospitals, a "vanilla" installation had more than 50 security groups. In the clinics, in a more complex access control environment, this same software package was installed with fewer than 30 security groups.

Academia

Universities also have a complex identity management environment that must manage the identities of academic staff, administrative staff, prospective students, enrolled students, researchers, and alumni. Researchers are particularly complex because they have both staff-like access requirements and student-like requirements. In addition, they have cross-institutional access control requirements because of the collaborative nature of their activity.

From an IAM perspective, possibly the most basic access required is by prospective students. This cohort is important because they have shown interest by accessing the university's website. At this point, while there is no need to register users, there are benefits from collecting email addresses. If users are given the opportunity to use social logins such as Google ID, Facebook, or Microsoft Live accounts, the university can commence promotion by sending appropriate course detail to them. This becomes a low-cost, low-impact mechanism for targeted marketing.

When a university student enrolls, a social login is no longer sufficient, and more information must be captured. A registration process is required, during which the appropriate identification documents must be viewed by an administrative person.

One area generally requiring attention by universities is learning management systems (LMSs). Since most university students these days are millennials, a focus on the LMS user experience is recommended. While the access control associated with an LMS is not trivial, the IdM environment should support this facility. Required information includes name, student number, enrollment status, subjects, and tutorial membership. The IdM system should provide this data, so that students need not navigate through multiple pages to find courses in their area of study. Also, the LMS will collect information such as workgroup memberships. This data should flow back to the IdP so that other applications can use it.

Note: Many universities are migrating to cloud-based LMSs. This makes it even more important to adopt a cloud-based strategy for the university's IdP (see chapter 5 for more detail).

Government

Government, too, has some non-trivial identity management requirements. In addition to staff, who might be employees or contractors, government must work with staff from external service providers. These are staff from organizations that provide services on behalf of government. For instance, in family services there might be a large cohort of social workers with access entitlement to the department's case management system. The identity management system should federate with the organization employing the social workers so that user credentials from their identity provider service can be used to manage their access entitlements.

On the citizen side, governments need the capability of accepting non-repudiable transactions for a government service. For instance, an online application form may need to be signed by an authorized company representative. The IdM system should be able to authenticate a user to the necessary level for the service being requested. For example, if a user's authentication level must be elevated, the IdM system needs access to the necessary identity document verification repositories to register the user at the required level of assurance.

It is necessary to establish the correct level of authentication assurance and match it to the registration process that users have gone through (see chapter 4 for more detail).

There is also a significant data sharing requirement within government. Often staff from multiple departments and agencies must work together and share document and files. Thus, the system needs a mechanism to securely share data cross-departmentally, as well as access to an IdM environment to determine the level of authentication a user who requests access to shared data should be given.

> On a recent assignment, staff from various agencies were surveyed in regard to their data sharing requirements. Police identified that when they dispatch a car to a residential address, if they knew someone at the address had mental health issues it would change the way they respond.
>
> The health department confirmed that it would be simple to flag addresses at which persons being treated for mental health illness reside. This would be for police purposes only, and the data would be anonymized.

Significant work is occurring within government to facilitate this requirement. The back-end attribute exchange (BAE) initiative[1] has established the core requirements for data exchange within government.

BAEs are particularly useful for physical access control whereby identity attributes are required in very distributed environments.

A Way Forward

Developing a KYC capability is an individualistic activity for an organization. It requires a knowledge of the customer base, a good understanding or the company's products and services, and a vision of the possibilities. One tool that can assist the planning and development of a competent KYC environment is a maturity assessment. It can accurately position the organization's KYC environment on a continuum from "chaotic" to "optimized." Once an accurate positioning has been determined, the organization can develop a program to reach the desired maturity level.

Maturity Model

A useful model to use when analyzing a KYC environment and planning its development is the five-level Carnegie Mellon Capability Maturity Model (CMM). Adapting this to KYC reveals the characteristics for each level, shown in Table 10.1.

---

[1] The Federated Identity, Credential, and Access Management (FICAM) BAE specification defines how a relying party could access data from an authoritative source established for attribute sharing.

Table 10.1: Carnegie Mellon Capability Maturity Model

Level	Description
Level 1: Chaotic	Processes are unpredictable and poorly controlled with no integration. The KYC efforts within the organization are ad hoc, are typically undocumented, and have been put in place to respond to audit failures and regulatory stimuli in the absence of any strategic management or architectural controls. There is no "centralization" of management and little communication between the various KYC initiatives.
Level 2: Reactive	Processes are managed but are reactive. Processes are typically documented with metrics in place, but this is largely because of the need to accommodate external stimuli over which there is little control. This level is characterized as "fighting fires" rather than managed response.
Level 3: Predictive	Processes are defined and managed. At this level, KYC process are integrated and part of the organization's business unit workflows. KYC information is used proactively for business enablement.
Level 4: Managed	KYC processes are mature and part of business operations. Services are both measured and controlled with capacity management in place. Costs are fully understood and accounted for, and KYC is provided to the business units under service-level agreement conditions.
Level 5: Optimized	Processes are optimized with a focus on continuous improvement. Automation analyzes KYC data with results reporting, regulatory and compliance reporting, and marketing initiatives occurring on schedule and at minimal cost. Staff research is facilitated, and there is a deep knowledge of the customer base.

Organizations should analyze the maturity of their KYC environments to determine their position on the continuum and decide on the desired position. They can then implement a development program to move to the desired level and plan their continual migration to higher levels as the business matures.

Once the requirements are known, a market scan of vendors in this space might be warranted. When selecting a vendor, it is important to have a prioritized list of requirements. High on the list should be scalability, since the consumer market is very broad, and a good user experience, because millennials require that.

Conclusion

We have focused on organizational issues with regard to consumerization, briefly considering the average consumer and how they might adapt to the changes that will come about.

It is quite clear that we are entering into a time of significant change in the delivery of customer services in the retail, corporate, and government sectors.

KYC programs will deliver an unprecedented level of sophistication in customer relations. However, this will require storage of an increasing amount of data on consumers and the transactions they undertake.

This begs the question, "how will the marketplace receive this requirement for increased data being stored about consumers?" Anecdotal evidence suggests that there are at least two considerations:

- Users will readily agree to providing their private data if they are adequately compensated for doing so. The "give-to-get" principle is appropriate here. Consumers will readily accept an offer that requires them to cede control over their privacy in direct relation to the utility of the offer. For instance, if a smartphone app requests access to the camera, GPS, and contacts, users will click "agree" if the app's utility is high.

- Users expect their data to be kept secure and for organizations that store their information to protect it. They don't want to have to understand this protection, and they don't want to be given any control over it—they just expect it. Organizations that fail to do this and as a consequence suffer a data loss will soon find it is not only their reputation that has suffered.

Use Case: AppliancePlus

Scenario	A white goods supplier, AppliancePlus, conducted a customer satisfaction survey and identified poor aftermarket service as a source of customer dissatisfaction. Research on appliance service websites confirmed that customers were having difficulty determining their service requirements, with several horror stories of consumers being poorly treated by service technicians.
Strategy	The product managers developed a common service approach for all AppliancePlus products and engaged their marketing department to develop a customer communication strategy for the company. This included a review of the products and services being provided by the company with a view to streamline customer transactions and improve the customer experience.
Solution	Service manuals were updated to be consistent across all products within each line of business; for example, all washing machine service manuals include the same sections, in the same order with the same level of detail. The website was expanded with a service portal that gave access to the manuals and provided service tips. Rather than use cookies, the website invited customers to register an account that accessed the sales record detail database to pre-populate the screen. Social logins were supported. A record of approved service technicians in the customer's area was provided based on the location indicated in the customer's record.

Q & A

Q. Most customer service improvement programs incur additional staff costs to provide the service. It then becomes hard to justify these costs against the economic benefit of the service improvement. How can service improvement be economically justified?

A. Justifying short-term benefits associated with improved customer service is not trivial, but it is possible. Some companies perform regular customer satisfaction surveys and subjectively equate changes to revenue. The cost of any change in customer satisfaction is offset against anticipated improvements in revenue. Another option is to conduct a pilot program and measure improved revenue for the pilot users against revenue improvements for non-participants.

Better still is to eliminate the need for additional staff via the use of automation and AI. By encoding service provision in an AI facility, user expectations are met with little recurring costs. This does not mean deploying a multi-level interactive voice response system that is typically despised by consumers. It means using the KYC facility to anticipate customer needs and then exceeding these needs by fully satisfying the requirement.

Those organizations that can do this are destined to experience increased prosperity, while those that don't are more likely to become digital transformation failures.

Q. Is there a danger that users will become anxious about the amount of data being accumulated and used by the KYC facility?

A. No. Customers are over the initial scare they got when they found out how much Google Chrome knew about the emails they had sent and blog posts they had made. Users expect organizations to intelligently use their information and provide them with efficient service. This means that multiple interactions with different service representatives during a single session should not require users to keep identifying themselves, giving their date of birth, or answering challenge-response questions.

Users appreciate it if you know the model number of the product they purchased from you and you connect them directly to the information on the unit, rather than having them navigate product selection screens that are often not intuitive or missing reference to the desired product model.

Q. Privacy legislation requires access to be given to organizations that maintain customer data. Isn't it better not to store this information in the first place?

A. No. KYC requires access to customer information that must be stored in a computer system. KYC is the future of business, and without it digital transformation will severely hamper a company's prosperity. There is therefore no option but to store increasing amounts of data against a customer's record in order to anticipate and satisfy their interaction with the company.

There are some other ramifications. Privacy legislation does constrain KYC programs that have not been planned strategically. Unless a customer has agreed to their data being shared within a business, there may be constraints on how that data can be used. For instance, if a customer purchases a product, they should be made aware that their details will be provided to the service management department for customer service purposes. This should also be stated in the company's privacy policy statement (see chapter 11 for more detail).

Privacy legislation might also require organizations to give customers access to the data being stored on them, and provide the ability for a customer to correct or annotate data in their customer records. This is made easier by a KYC facility that, by definition, should integrate all the data being kept on a customer. It is important that privacy be factored into the development of a KYC facility.

Chapter 11

Regulation: It Makes Sense

There are multiple facets to cybersecurity, many of them going well beyond the focus and capacity of this book. Identity management, however, has a direct impact on the security of identity data and regulatory controls over the collection, storage, and usage of identity information.

As we become more connected, organizations, both commercial and public sector, will increasingly store more data about us. This will be driven by the desire of companies to understand us so that they can sell us more products and services, and by governments that want to leverage their identity information to adopt a "digital first" strategy for providing services. As these organizations extend their data repositories, the general public expects this data to be adequately managed to protect their privacy. However, members of the public are becoming increasingly scared because they know systems are vulnerable and they doubt the capability of organizations, particularly government, to adequately protect it.

Organizations can therefore expect more, not less, regulation. Rather than resist this, we need to embrace it, plan for it, and deploy systems that are compliant. As with most regulatory issues, this needs to be done this before it has to be done.

Cybersecurity

To the uninitiated, the term *cybersecurity* is a nebulous concept that appears to embody a wide variety of products and processes. To those in the business, it is often used as an umbrella term that lacks any specific meaning. But the essence of cybersecurity is quite simple and, with a little direction, can be useful in determining what should be done in terms of online protection of customers and citizens.

A useful framework for the development of a cybersecurity strategy is the Confidentiality-Integrity-Availability (CIA) model, shown in Table 11.1.

Table 11.1: CIA model

Element	Description
Confidentiality	This element requires protection to be in place to ensure that sensitive or private data is not made available, either intentionally or inadvertently, to persons who should not have it. This could be corporate intellectual property such as patented product design documents, company-sensitive information such as product development plans, or files containing customer data. A company's cybersecurity strategy must explicitly address how information is to be kept confidential; part of this will be how the company is ensuring adherence to privacy legislation within its jurisdiction(s) of operation.
Integrity	Organizations are obligated to ensure that the data they hold measures up to a requirement for integrity. This means that they must put effort into ensuring that data is accurate and up to date. This simply makes sense; if a company is making decisions using inaccurate data, mistakes will be made. Also, if an organization releases information that is found to be inaccurate, consequences will result. In the identity space, privacy legislation in most developed countries requires that data is regularly updated, or deleted. To fail to maintain the integrity of personal information could have significant consequences.
Availability	There are at least two aspects of availability that a cybersecurity framework should address: *what* availability should be provided (i.e., who can access what) and *how* availability should be provided (i.e., what access mechanisms should be put in place). The "what" variable would normally involve the adoption of a classification methodology to ensure the organization knows what information types it has, so that it can determine the level of protection that each should be afforded. Most organizations adopt a four-level classification scheme, such as top-secret, confidential, internal, and unrestricted (see chapter 9 for more detail). The "how" variable should address access mechanisms such as the requirement for an API to secure access to protected data, and scalability issues such as the need to aggregate logs across multiple servers.

Cybersecurity Devices

There are two broad categories of devices for cybersecurity protection: intrusion detection systems (IDSs) and data loss prevention (DLP) systems.

Intrusion Detection

IDSs comprise a class of systems that either sits as a gateway device on a corporate network to stop intrusion attempts, or sits on the network and monitors traffic for behavioral pattern analysis. Gateway functionality is sometimes incorporated into load-balancing equipment. These devices monitor traffic to identify any nefarious activity. Behavioral analytics devices on the network use artificial intelligence (AI) to build an "understanding" of normal network behavior to allow abnormalities, such as hacker activity, to be identified, notified, and investigated.

There are two broad categories:

- Monitoring systems—An intrusion detection device that monitors network traffic to detect intrusion attempts is designed to identify possible attacks external to the organization and stop them from doing damage. These are typically network-level devices that monitor for specific events such as denial of service (DoS) or man-in-the-middle attacks (i.e., spoofing of login details or certificates). Another task that these devices are increasingly being required to provide is monitoring for signature matches for ransomware attacks, using either commercially available or publicly available attack vector details[1].

- Analyzing systems—Another type of system, becoming more commonplace, is the IDS that analyzes traffic on the network in order to identify misuse from internal users.

  Such analyzing systems are also becoming important for identifying network compromise via an account hijack. If a hacker uses a phishing attack to obtain the access credentials for a user's account, an analyzing system will likely be able to identify unusual account activity and initiate account suspension.

Data Loss Prevention

While IDSs are more concerned with keeping nefarious behavior out, DLP systems are concerned with keeping protected data in. Although the two approaches intersect with the need to stop exfiltration—that is, data leaving the

---

[1] The STIX and TAXII initiatives provide for the definition of attacks and a reference database of known signatures to be considered as a component of cybersecurity strategy development.

corporate network, DLP systems have some unique properties. Again, there are two broad categories:

- Network DLP—Network solutions range from basic network devices that sit at the edge of a network and monitor traffic for embargoed keywords, to sophisticated devices that "learn" what network traffic normally looks like on the corporate network and raise alarms when this changes. For instance, if a person who normally accesses the previous month's corporate board documents once a month downloads multiple board meeting minutes all at once, a notification would be generated, and the account may be suspended pending investigation.

- Endpoint DLP—Endpoint solutions are typically software products that sit on client devices, or endpoint servers, and monitor activity. They often employ rights management to determine whether or not a requestor has the appropriate access rights to a file or document.

  In some cases, endpoint monitoring is achieved by downloading an "agent" on the client's device that monitors activity and reports back to a DLP device on the network.

An organization's framework for cybersecurity should analyze its requirement for such protection and select a solution that best fits the requirement.

Regulation Summary

The major regulations that affect data security are as follows:

PCI

The payment card industry (PCI) provides guidelines on the correct treatment of information such as credit card details and provides an auditable standard. It is most important that, as e-commerce continues to grow, organizations safeguard their credit card information handling to avoid revenue loss from repudiated transactions and violation penalties. Payment gateways must adhere to PCI guidelines and submit to periodic audits.

HIPAA

The purpose of the US Health Insurance Portability and Accountability Act (HIPAA) is to protect health information. While the main focus of health information protection has been embodied in personal health record controls, HIPAA goes beyond that to set regulation for security controls that manage access to protected health information. It stipulates how hospitals and health centers should ensure protection of sensitive data.

SOX

The Sarbanes-Oxley Act (SOX) in the US does not directly impinge on data privacy. It does seek to regulate, and provide useful guidelines for, corporate governance, including auditor independence and the need to disclose data loss that has detrimental effects.

FERPA

The Family Education Rights and Privacy Act (FERPA) seeks to manage public schools and colleges in the US and provides a framework for any educational jurisdiction to follow in the collection and management of student education records.

GLBA

The Gramm-Leach Bliley Act (GLBA) forms part of privacy regulation in the US and provides guidelines for the control of personal information, particularly in the financial industry. Banks, insurance, and wealth management companies are covered by the GLBA, which requires them to implement safeguards in regard to client personal information.

Privacy and Data Protection

Some countries have focused legislation specifically on privacy of sensitive data, while others have addressed privacy in the wider context of data protection.

Definition

The concept of privacy is quite broad. We all think we know what it means, but there are many viewpoints as to how best to define it. Although there are dictionary definitions of what it is, it is more meaningful to define what it means:

Privacy is the desire of individuals to control, or influence, the collection, usage, and disclosure of data about themselves.

The following terms are related to privacy, and need definition in their own right:

- Confidentiality—seeks to control the release of identity data
- Secrecy—is the intentional concealment of identity data
- Anonymity—is the ability to conceal identity data

Privacy is largely a Western construct, and even among the developed countries there is wide divergence on the desire for privacy and toleration of its violation. In many Western European countries, particularly those that have experienced occupation during wartime, the desire for privacy is tempered by the desire for efficiency of government services. In other countries such as the US and the UK, there is a skepticism of government and its ability to keep identity information private. In these geographies, privacy is highly regarded, and efficiency of government services will typically be subjugated to privacy protection.

Principles

Most privacy legislation has at its core certain principles that, if followed, will keep user information private and avoid contravention of privacy legislation, with its attendant costs. Table 11.2 lists these principles.

Table 11.2: Privacy principles

Principle	Description
Policy	Organizations that collect personally identifiable information (PII) should publish a policy that states how the organization collects, stores, and uses such information. Instruction must be provided regarding how an individual may gain access to the organization's information to validate its accuracy. Instruction should be provided regarding how an individual may lodge a complaint about the information that is kept on them and how the organization will deal with such complaints, including expected timeframes.

Collection of data	Organizations may only collect PII data that is required for a specific transaction. They can't collect data that they "might need in the future" or collect extra data for marketing purposes unless they expressly state that, and seek the subject's consent. This means that, if an organization wants to use transaction data for big data analysis for marketing purposes, they must de-identify it.
	A common violation of privacy policy is committed by software testers when they use a client database for test purposes, often in the cloud. In such an instance, the identity data should be obfuscated by randomizing first and last names, address detail, and phone numbers.
	When collecting data, the organization must ensure that informed user consent is collected; that is, advice as to the stated use of the information must be provided.
	If a transaction does not need the explicit identification of a user, there must be the option of completing a transaction anonymously or with a pseudonym.
Disclosure of personal information	It is forbidden for organizations to disclose PII to other organizations, or even other divisions within the same organization, unless expressly agreed to by the subject. This means that if a bank collects PII for the purpose of opening a bank account, they cannot provide this information to their insurance branch without the subject's express permission.
Cross-border disclosure	Organizations that store PII information on citizens of the country in which they undertake business must not store the information in a jurisdiction that does not have legislation at least as stringent as in the home country. For instance, if a call center is established in a low-cost jurisdiction that has weaker privacy legislation, the organization must deploy specific controls to ensure the privacy of persons in the data file used by call center representatives.

Principle	Description	Table 11.2 continued
Use of government identifiers	There are constraints on the use of government identifiers as an index on data files. For instance, a department of motor vehicles might use a driver's license number as an index, but another department should not use driver's license numbers as an index for their data stores. Equally, commercial organizations that collect driver's license numbers (e.g., car rental companies) should create their own index fields and not use driver's license numbers for this purpose. This does not preclude the use of a driver's license number to locate a user record.	
Quality of PII data	Organizations that collect PII data must take steps to maintain its currency. Once a data record has passed its date of currency, there are two options: the company must engage resources to validate its accuracy and correct it if it's wrong, or it must delete the data record. The date of refresh should be stated in the organization's privacy policy. However, it's generally agreed that address data is sufficiently out of date after three years.	
Security of PII data	Organizations must deploy appropriate security measures, commensurate with the sensitivity of the data in question. Data must be protected from misuse, interference, unauthorized access, modification, and disclosure. This includes data backups and files used for testing purposes. A related control is the necessity to delete or destroy PII information that is no longer needed; it's not permissible to maintain a data file containing PII data just because it might be of use in the future.	
Access and correction of PII data	If an entity holds personal information about an individual, the entity must, on request by the individual, give them access to the information. This means that processes must be established to facilitate access, and correction processes should be published in the organization's policy statement with an indication of the timeframe that the subject should expect for a response. If the subject of a record containing PII data requests correction of a data element, it must either be changed or annotated.	

While an initial reaction might be that these requirements are onerous, they do in fact make good sense. Organizations are well advised to adopt these principles and avoid the cost and embarrassment of data loss that might otherwise occur.

What Some Countries Are Doing

Privacy legislation across Westernized countries differs widely. It seems that there are three broad stages through which such legislation processes:

- First generation—privacy statements are published by governments with constraints on government departments and agencies to adhere to the principles.

- Second generation—privacy legislation is enacted that obligates commercial organizations to adhere to the legislation but without the stipulation of significant legal penalty.

- Third generation—privacy legislation is well defined, and clearly indicates the letter and spirit of the law, with significant and enforceable penalty.

A subjective view of the status of privacy legislation in some Western geographies is as follows:

United States

There is no single all-encompassing privacy legislation in the US. The basis for legislation is the Fourth Amendment of the Constitution, which gives citizens the right to be free of unwarranted search or seizure, and the Fourteenth Amendment, which affords a general right to privacy. While there is correlation between the Constitution and specific industry regulation, in the US the legislative "teeth" are ensconced in either specific state legislation or industry-specific regulation.

At the federal level, specific rights are spelled out in various industry-specific legislation, such as SOX and GLBA, both of which are focused on the financial sector; FERPA in the education sector; and HIPAA in health care.

At the state level, Article 1 of the California Constitution stipulates that privacy is an inalienable right. In Florida, similar legislation is in place with Article 1 restricting government intervention in a person's life. Montana specifically references privacy as a right in Article 2 of its constitution.

There are some specific privacy issues addressed in state legislation, such as the California Reader Privacy Act and the Washington State protection of text messaging. Search without a warrant is expressly prohibited.

At this time, a subjective scoring of US legislation would be Generation 1.5. It is unlikely that an action against violation of privacy would succeed unless a deliberate and specific law violation could be proven.

Europe

The European General Data Protection Regulation (GDPR) represents the world's "best practice" privacy legislation, and can be considered Generation 3 legislation: actionable and possessing teeth. It achieves two things:

- Centralization of 28 different privacy regulatory environments into one, which simplifies adherence to privacy legislation for companies operating in Europe.

- Providing "teeth"—significant, enforceable penalties—to the legislation, which are generally missing in other jurisdictions.

The legislation means that organizations that collect identity data must ensure that good security practices are in place, that an evaluation of the data being stored on persons is understood and appropriate, and that good records management is established and maintained. These are all desirable outcomes; the existence of a big stick is secondary. Given that the stick exists, it makes little sense for companies to focus on maximizing sales and minimizing costs in order to drive profit, without expending appropriate effort on avoiding privacy legislation violation.

The legislation provides EU citizens better access to, and control of, their identity data being kept by European legal entities. It means that most companies will need to undertake some operational and system changes to provide this access and to accommodate instances in which a person's view of their identity data, and the company's view, diverge.

Items of note are:

- PII must be treated appropriately, which means that its confidentiality must be protected with processes in place to prevent access to the data and the equipment on which it is stored.

- The network on which personal data is communicated must have protection in place to resist malicious attacks and avoid inadvertent release of information. The availability, authenticity, integrity, and confidentiality of stored or transmitted personal data must be protected to a defined level of confidence.

- A person who is the subject of a data record must be able to evaluate and potentially contest a decision that has been made on the basis of a data record, even if the determination is machine-generated.

It is likely that the European GDPR legislation will become the model for future privacy legislation, particularly in jurisdictions with trade arrangements with

Europe. It significantly informed the Safe Harbors replacement guidelines in the drafting of the EU-US Privacy Shield principles.

China

China has made nascent steps in regulating personal data. The Constitution, as adopted by the Fifth National People's Congress in 1982, does address basic protection of people's data by state employees with punishment of up to three years in jail for any violation.

While the Constitution does not explicitly define personal information, it can be a "secret" (i.e., information not normally made available). The Telecom and Internet Users Personal Data Protection Regulation defines personal information as

> *"Users' names, dates of birth, identity card number, address, telephone number, account number, password and other information with which the identity of the user can be distinguished independently or in combination with other information, as well as the time, and place of the user using the service and other information."*

Telecom operators must keep such information secure and abide by the "principles of legality, propriety, and necessity."

From a Western perspective, privacy protection in China is subjectively evaluated at Gen 1.0.

Singapore

Singapore was an early adopter of data protection regulation with the Personal Data Protection Commission established to administer the Personal Data Protection Act 2012 (PDPA).

The act stipulates that consent must be obtained before personal data is collected and used. It is incumbent on companies to ensure that customers or clients are told how their information is to be used so that they can give "informed" consent.

Singapore legislation aims to balance the needs of organizations against the needs of individuals. It relies on the "reasonableness test": what would a reasonable person do in a specific situation? While this is practical, it does introduce a level of subjectivity in any legal action that an aggrieved person might bring. The PDPA is considered to be at a Gen 2.5 level.

Hong Kong

Hong Kong was an early adopter of privacy regulation, when it initially released the Personal Data Ordinance in 1995, two years before the handover to China.

The ordinance comprises six principles that govern the collection, use, and retention of personal data; data security; openness to data subjects; and correction processes. Data is defined quite broadly to include information that "directly or indirectly" relates to the identity of a living person.

While the 2011 amendment tightened regulation regarding corporate use of customer's data, particularly in regard to direct marketing campaigns, and added a process whereby aggrieved persons can access legal assistance in meritorious cases, the legislation can only be considered Gen 2.0. Compensation levels for aggrieved parties are quite low, the ordinance favors legal interpretation that should not be difficult for a lawyer to argue, and there is a growing political influence in Hong Kong in which privacy is low on the agenda. Hong Kong is possibly at Gen 2.0.

Australia

The situation in Australia changed in 2014 when the Privacy Act amendment (2012) came into force. The amendment extended the Act to include restrictions on direct marketing, access by individuals to their data records, and stringent rules regarding correction of data. Even if an organization disagrees with a user's contention that data is in error, the organization must provide a written reason for their disagreement and must annotate the person's record in their data store to indicate that it has been contested.

A major shortcoming of the previous legislation was corrected by giving the Commissioner the ability to initiate action in the event of a violation of privacy legislation—in other words, there's no need to wait for a complaint to be lodged.

Australia's privacy legislation can be considered Gen 2.5.

Industry Regulation

There are three industries in which significant regulation has been enacted. For any company operating in these industries, it is worthwhile to consider the specific regulation in force within the jurisdictions in which they operate.

Health Care

Possibly one of the most regulated industries, from a privacy perspective, is health care. Specific controls are placed on operators to avoid inadvertent disclosure of sensitive data; this goes beyond the release of PII to the release of disease information or even just the knowledge that a procedure has occurred. The major initiatives to protect health care data have been in the electronic health record (EHR) area, which has been deployed to varying degrees in most Western countries. This make sense because having the ability to share information about previous procedures could make new procedures redundant. This could potentially save significant money that would otherwise be spent on repeating tests and related procedures. It also contributes to the provision of longitudinal care whereby a patient's health journey is assessed rather than relying on a single acute care procedure.

While there is no specific EHR regulation for all jurisdictions to follow, it is incumbent on health care professionals to ensure that EHR deployments meet health care regulation within their jurisdiction(s) of operation. This will involve the protection of an individual's health data in accordance with the "consent" that has been granted by the patient. Data that has been marked as to be only available to specific health professionals must not be released beyond that cohort unless extraordinary conditions exist, in which case appropriate notifications must be made. Giving patients control of the use and release of their medical records is an important part of patient identity management.

HIPAA was implemented in 1996 and is the grandfather of health regulation. The intent is to allow the flow of health information needed to provide and promote high-quality health care while ensuring that individuals' health information is properly protected. It stipulates constraints on the use and disclosure of "protected health information" by entities subject to the "privacy rule." Protected health information is health information that's individually identifiable. Data that is de-identified—for the purposes of disease control analysis, for instance—is not covered. The Privacy Rule constrains covered entities that hold or transmit protected health information.

HIPAA is much broader than EHR controls; in fact, EHR comes under the HIPAA umbrella. Health care facilities hold much more data than is available via EHR systems. For instance, most hospital patient administration systems have patient health details that are not included in patient EHR entries and must therefore be protected from inadvertent, or malicious, release.

It is noted that there is a tension between clinicians and privacy regulators. Health care professionals want unrestricted access to longitudinal patient care data. If a patient presents at a clinic, reference to patient history will likely improve patient care. If a patient presents at an acute care facility, recent procedures at a clinic will likely inform the clinician regarding appropriate health care. But controls must be placed on this access to information, and, when a patient presents, they should be given with the necessary instruction to allow them to provide informed consent to the access and release of their prior health care information.

Financial

When the global financial crisis of 2007–2008 hit, the result was always going to be increased regulation of the financial industry. Banks have borne the brunt of this increased regulation, but other financial institutions and insurance companies have also been affected. Regulation such as MiFID rules, Basel III, EOIPA's Solvency II guidelines, and the Volcker Rule are all now constraining banking and financial services company operations. But that is not the focus here; we are interested in the effect of banking regulation on personal identity data and how the financial services industry could take an increasingly central role in the management of a person's identity information.

When it comes to regulation of account holder privacy for banks or insurance companies, the picture in the US is quite complex. Most banks now publish their own policy documents that detail how they protect an account holder's privacy. The Federal Deposit Insurance Corporation has issued privacy guidelines to ensure that financial institutions address the topic of privacy. They must publish, and annually review, a privacy policy statement, and they have adopted a "privacy rule" approach that requires banks to adhere to a basic set of principles in their treatment of account holder information. It is incumbent on banks to allow account holders to opt out of any data sharing, although this does not include the sharing of data between affiliated parties. The GLBA requires banks to explain their information-sharing practices to their customers and to safeguard the PII of their customers that they hold.

Utilities

There is now heavy regulation of utilities, and a utility company must stay abreast of developments in this space. There are two aspects of import in the area of identity management, shown in Table 11.3.

Table 11.3: Identity management issues for the utilities industry

Issue	Description
Internal access control to utility infrastructure	There are two drivers of change in the area of access to infrastructure: The Internet of Things (IoT) is dramatically changing the face of operational technology, as prices of devices drop substantially, and innovative software to collect and share data is becoming readily available. Managing device access control requires a robust identity provider service that can respond to access control requests and evaluate a user's entitlement for access to a collected data set or to issue controls to an actuator (see chapter 9 for more detail). Operational networks that have in the past been separated from IT are now being integrated so that they can access current identity data in order to make access control decisions.
Privacy of customer information	As with other public-facing industries, utility companies must protect customer data and adhere to privacy regulation in the jurisdiction in which they work. They also can act as an identity provider service for their clients. As governments increasingly support third-party identity providers in public access to government services, utilities have the ability to provide such a service. In comparison to other organizations, utilities have the most up-to-date address records since they maintain service addresses for their utilities.

Note there is specific regulation in place for electricity grid operators under the North American Electric Reliability Corporation (NERC), which sets guidelines for transmission utilities to follow. In some circumstances, operators will not be able to integrate their operation and informational networks and will need to maintain "air gaps" for perceived safety reasons (see chapter 8 for more detail). This will hamper their ability to leverage the organization's identity provider service for access control purposes.

Conclusion

Regulation has several facets. On the one hand, we tend to resent regulation and criticize our governments for creating the "nanny state." On the other hand, we decry the lack of regulation when we hear of preventable accidents in third-world countries that lack the regulation we have. But we need a balance: regulation should be "appropriate." This means that we want to impose regulation in a measured and considered fashion, not have it imposed as a result of a catastrophe that could have been avoided.

A case in point is IoT regulation that is not keeping up with technology. It is likely an accident is imminent. Draconian regulation will follow, and we have only ourselves to blame.

Use Case: Finco Bank

Scenario	Finco Bank has a large back-office operation that has served it well over the years but is increasingly a hindrance to digital transformation. As each new regulation—from capital ratios to anti-money laundering (AML)—has come about, bolt-on solutions to the core banking applications have been developed. The result is a fragmented repository of customer information and an inability to form a single view of a customer's business and touchpoints with the bank.
Strategy	Finco Bank has embarked on a core-systems replacement program whereby multiple customer data stores are to be integrated. This will allow a single view of a customer's information. The bank can then embark on development to move from KYC for AML purposes to a truly valuable database of customer information. This database can allow the bank to leverage its identity store to drive new business opportunities and introduce new innovative services.
Solution	A central customer database was designed and a product selected that provides for multiple interfaces to support multiple relying applications. Under the new system, all account provisioning was centralized to the customer database, and connectors were deployed that either supported a real-time lookup or, for legacy applications, synchronized data to and from the relying system. This allowed the bank to record all transactions in the database and run analytics on a periodic basis, to build a value-based matrix that identified high-net-worth individuals (HNWIs) and prospective HNWIs. The system was also used as a core repository for an AI system to answer customer queries about the probability of success of and interest rates offered for a mortgage application.

Q & A

Q. How can cross-jurisdictional businesses keep up with the privacy legislation in multiple geographies?

A. In most situations where multiple jurisdictions must be accommodated, the most stringent requirement should drive the needs. For an enterprise with European, USA, and Asia Pacific requirements, the GDPR guidelines should be followed.

By following the principles above and developing a corporate approach to privacy regulation, most jurisdictional requirements will be satisfied, and only exceptions would need to be considered. This can be accomplished by having a privacy consultant from the pertinent jurisdictions review the privacy strategy and highlight any conditional constraints.

Adherence to privacy regulation should not be considered onerous; it should be considered best practice in order to protect PII and avoid any consequences that might have cost or embarrassment impacts.

Q. In the health care sector, is the EHR sufficient to protect a patient's privacy?

A. No. Health care organizations must review all repositories of patient data and ensure that adequate protection is in place. While the EHR system is a major step forward in the protection of a patient's health information, if a medical center receptionist has access to the patient administration system that contains sensitive information on a patient's visit, it's likely that HIPPA and privacy regulation have been violated.

Q. A person's credit rating is made by a ratings company, so the data is "owned" by the institution and is not captured by privacy regulation—correct?

A. No. If the rating is applicable to an individual, the person has the right to access the information. In Europe, an individual also has the right to disclosure of the algorithm that was used to determine the rating. In Australia, a person has the right for a contested rating to be annotated with their version of events that led to the rating.

The "enlightened" company will use such regulation to their advantage, either developing an appropriate relationship with the customer or using a contested rating to sever the relationship with a customer.

Chapter 12

A Forward Glance

Gazing into the future is always a bit of fun. Some people do it for a living and are called futurists. A futurist is generally working at a high level, such as driverless cars or supersonic transport, both of which we are likely to see widely deployed in our lifetimes. But when it comes to the future of IAM, we need to be a bit more precise. Some things are obvious—for instance, we need to get a lot better at managing staff identities. Since many staff are not employees, federated authentication will become more important. We need to be able to trust the identity provider services of a partner organization and to adequately audit their registration processes.

How we will accommodate other trends is not so clear. We know consumerization is upon us and that we need to be able to massively scale our identity management environments, but exactly how to do so, and to know what's important, remains a little fuzzy. In fact, there's a movement in academia that posits it's not what you know about your customers that's important, it's what you don't know.

They point out that for all the massive big data analysis that goes into identifying trends, it becomes extremely difficult to draw conclusions. Just because a large percentage of a particular demographic bought something does not mean that they are going to continue to do so. The demographics are not the causal agent; they are just part of the observation. No matter how strong the correlation, there's always a degree of uncertainty about predicting the future based on history. The need, therefore, is to "know your customer's jobs to be done"[1]—that is, get to know what your customers want and then set about providing it.

But we can be sure that one of the biggest growth areas will be in managing customer identities. Customers are becoming more discerning and will not tolerate a poor experience. Unlike the baby boomers who demand low prices and high value, millennials value experience. The experience they receive on a website trumps value; if they don't get it, they will walk—and tweet as they do.

---

[1] *Harvard Business Review*, September 2016

Data Privacy

The whole area of data privacy is going to change. Up-to-date approaches to protect sensitive identity data have to be adopted and coordinated. This is because, by definition, protecting someone's private data hinders the sorts of things we can do with it. If data must be stored in a protected area, it will be more difficult to work with. For this reason, many companies and governments have paid lip service to data privacy and have not achieved anything substantial in the way of data privacy protection. While we have a great deal of privacy regulation, most countries have enacted legislation that dictates measures to be taken when dealing with sensitive data on their country's citizens. But generally such legislation has no teeth: it is written by lawyers who would have little difficulty in successfully arguing against any prosecution, and penalties are typically not clearly defined. An exception is the GDPR legislation in Europe, which is a wakeup call for industry.

> A recent attempt to download an app from Google Play revealed that it requested access to a number of services such as the camera, GPS data, contacts, and photo gallery, which had no bearing whatsoever on the app. Increasingly, sophisticated users will not tolerate this abuse and will refuse to download such apps. Developers will pull the app because of poor adoption rates, and the development costs will be wasted, all because of a lack of governance over the app development process.

There is little doubt that legislation will improve and that companies that fail to protect themselves are increasingly exposing their companies to risk. Collecting sensitive information on staff, business partners, and customers means that a few simple rules should be observed:

- Don't collect more information than is necessary in order to complete a transaction. Collecting data because it might be useful in the future exposes the organization to a greater risk and is illegal in most Western jurisdictions.
- Don't use data that has been collected for one purpose, for another. This means that if a bank collects data on a customer when they open a bank account, and the bank then passes information to their insurance branch for follow-up, the bank is breaking the law, unless they have specifically asked the customer's permission to do so.

- Protect sensitive data. The storage repository that contains the database or directory of people's identity data should be adequately secured. This will typically involve a combination of encryption, stringent control on those who can access to the directory, and some form of privileged account management for system administrators who require access to the database for maintenance purposes. It also means that backup data sets must also be appropriately protected.

> At one identity audit for an Australian medical center, it was observed that they had run out of space for their hard copy patient files and were storing the files on a high shelf that extended around the waiting room!

- Ensure that jurisdictional restrictions are observed. Most privacy legislation restricts storage of data on the country's citizens in another country, unless that country has the same level of protection on stored data. This means that a utility that moves their call center to a low-cost jurisdiction must investigate the privacy legislation in the target country before establishing a customer database in that country. Note: It is expected that this requirement will diminish in importance as cloud service providers improve their offerings. From a technical point of view, it is immaterial where a secure database is stored these days.

- Provide a user access to their data so that they can verify it and correct it, if necessary. In the event of a disagreement, a notation should be placed on the user's record to indicate that the user had contested the validity of the disputed data.

Following a few basic guidelines not only reduces the probability of a challenge via privacy legislation, it reduces the chance of a breach and heightens the chance that a customer will have a good experience in dealing with your company. Since the technology is readily available to achieve these requirements, there is no excuse for managers who continue to expose their companies to unnecessary risk.

Data Ownership

We can expect some seminal changes in the definition of who owns data. People are becoming increasingly savvy in regard to collection of data and will start to assert what they consider to be their "rights" when it comes to storing data on their activities.

Telcos

When a telephone call is made, the telephone company records the time the call began, the number called, and the call's duration. Who owns the data? The telcos consider that they do, and of course, they need this data for billing purposes and network planning activities. But increasingly customers will want this data treated in accordance with privacy legislation and to be potentially recompensed for its use. In response, telcos argue that the information is de-identified (i.e., it contains no names or sensitive data); but the telephone number is an identity attribute, and it's not difficult to cross-reference it to glean sensitive data. The whole issue becomes even more important for telcos that provide Internet services, with browsing history becoming very valuable for marketing purposes.

Retail

The collection and analysis of data on the purchasing habits of customers is increasingly a big business for large retail organizations. Innovative loyalty programs track customer behavior and allow retailers to significantly improve their business by offering target promotions to customers who have a propensity to purchase. For instance, if a grocery store knows a customer is a regular coffee drinker, the store can:

- Offer a price reduction on the customer's preferred coffee to bring them back into the store.

- Use the information in a sales promotion for another coffee supplier to negotiate a more lucrative supplier agreement.

- Use the information to drive sales in an adjacent product category, such as coffee creamers or sugar substitutes.

But who owns this information? Increasingly retail organizations should seek to recompense customers for the use of this information and enter into a "pact" whereby the retailer is given permission to use the data for marketing purposes in exchange for discounts on preferred products or cash for offers available only to program members who agree to participate in the offer. There are significant benefits for retailers associated with such win-win situations.

Medical

Ownership of medical data is even more convoluted. Generally speaking, medical personnel consider that they own patient data. General practitioners, who generally maintain a patient's longitudinal data record, consider patient data to be theirs and are even resistant to contributing it to the patient's electronic health record over which patients have control. For acute care facilities, medical personnel consider that data collected by medical staff with hospital or clinic equipment belongs to them.

The net result is that hospitals, medical centers, clinics, and pharmacies are generally quite poor at protecting patient data. Access control and data retention practices vary widely across health jurisdictions. Often the necessary policy is not being established to ensure that adequate data management practices are in place. This means that even as patients assume their records are confidential, doctors in one location can access health records from another; reception staff can view sensitive patient medical data that is not required for them to perform their jobs; and test results, assumed to be held in strict confidence, are stored in low-security areas within community clinics.

> A recent conversation with a IT manager in a department of health indicated the scale of data ownership issues in healthcare. He was asked how patient Fitbit data was being managed. "It isn't," was his response. "We don't own the device, so we can't import the data and store it."

Management of medical data is now getting the attention it deserves, as patient consent systems are being deployed in most developing countries. The two main drivers for these initiatives are the poor record of medical institutions in protecting patient data, and the recognition that medical costs are escalating because best practices such as sharing of test results is often inadequate. Most jurisdictions are now implementing electronic health record (EHR) systems that correct these shortcomings and ensure patients give consent to the release of their medical data. When a comprehensive EHR system is in place, hospitals and medical centers can implement tighter security on their patient data to ensure that it is only made available on a need-to-know basis in accordance with policy.

Consumer Rights

Consumerization is a major trend that will have a profound effect on our lives over the next few years. It will be most noticeable in the retail sector, but institutions such as banks and utility companies will also dramatically improve their interaction with consumers. These organizations will seek to personalize their customer service and streamline the user experience when consumers engage via their online or in-person channels. This will require major changes in the way organizations manage consumer data. While in the past most members of the public have taken a blasé approach to managing their online identity information, this is changing. Although customers want website operation to be easy and will trade ease of use against data privacy, they expect their data to be protected and treated appropriately. The complexity of technology and lack of understanding of data protection options doesn't mean that expectations are any lower. Organizations should have customer rights at heart and should ensure that the data consumers entrust to companies is treated appropriately. Issues that will amplify these consumer rights issues are:

- Recent large losses of sensitive data by organizations that didn't maintain adequate protection, which resulted in significant costs or damage to reputation. Publication of these events and their aftermath elevate user awareness and the desire for improvements in data protection practices.

- Internet of Things (IoT) and the ubiquitous nature of identity information. For instance, in a world in which an automobile automatically provides owner identity data when it's driven into a service center, there are privacy issues. When a shopping mall knows when a customer enters the premises and knows their purchasing habits, there's a privacy issue. When a person gives a cleaner online access to their house door lock, privacy issues arise.

- Increased concern about the storage of identity data by governments and organizations, with the realization that data joining between these entities could cause reputation or more economic harm.

Consumers will increasingly become suspicious of any activity that seeks to gather data on their identity, interests, or purchasing preferences. They will resist supplying this data and will actively discourage others from doing so. Websites must seek to build relationships with customers to get them to contribute in a mutually beneficial way. The "give to get" principle should be followed, with consumers compensated for their involvement and for contributing their data to the information base that will benefit both the company and the participants.

Increasingly customers will be seeking experience rather than value. Whereas baby boomers are fixated on getting a good deal, millennials are looking for experience. They will gladly pay to get a better haircut, to buy the same shirt as their friends, or to purchase the right deodorant. When they are on your website, they want to be treated with respect and have the site work efficiently, which means that the site will need to maintain some type of identity data. This is not of concern, provided the site works first time, every time and in some way compensates them for their patronage. As noted in chapter 6, websites must be responsive because most site access by millennials will be from a smartphone.

Companies that fail to do this will run afoul of the power of social networking. Whereas in the past marketing strategists advised that a satisfied customer would tell seven associates and dissatisfied customers would tell 11 associates, it's now at least an order of magnitude different. It is easy for hundreds, if not thousands of people to hear about poor customer service or abuse of supplier power.

Government Services

Governments face a conundrum. They know the power of online facilities and want to follow a "digital first" strategy whereby services are released online before other channels, such as a call center or face-to-face customer service center. This has led some jurisdictions such as the US and the UK to establish an authentication environment that is transient—that is, there is no persistent storage of identity data by the government. In the scenarios, multiple providers of identity are established and accredited to operate within the government's authentication environment. Citizens then select one supplier to provide their identity provider service and establish an account that matches the assurance level required by the government service. It is noted that programs such as these are expensive to establish and maintain because the government must establish policy, set up accreditation schemes, and possibly provide financial support to service providers.

Smaller jurisdictions such as many European countries as well as countries in Asia and Oceania have elected to leverage their existing repositories of citizen data to provide an authentication to government online services. Often these data repositories are spread across multiple agencies. The department of motor vehicles typically has the largest repository of citizen data, since this organization typically accounts for over half of all transactions with the public. Health, education, and social services also maintain significant identity data stores. The task of government is to harmonize the data in these stores and the registration processes that create them. The health department will not "trust" an identity from the department of education unless it has been through a registration process with the same rigor as its own.

In some cases, a combination of public identity providers (IdPs) such as Google ID or Microsoft Live is used for low-assurance transactions, such as the purchase of a fishing permit. But as soon as higher-assurance authentication is required— to access a person's driving record, for instance, an identity verification process such as a 100-point check must be followed. The results must then be stored in the user's IdP record, be it a third-party data store or the government's own persistent identity record.

Increasingly government services require non-repudiation of a transaction. This adds another complexity with a two-factor authentication typically required. This means that the identity store must record the necessary attributes for this to occur, be it the citizen's cell number, fingerprint template, voice print, or facial recognition template.

Identity Provider Services

There will be a significant increase in provision of identity provider services. This will be driven by the two major trends in identity management: consumerization and IoT. Consumerization will fuel the need for third-party identity providers to authenticate members of the public and manage their identity data over the coming years. IoT will drive the fear of making too much data available. More and more, automobiles, houses, and fridges will want to "personalize" their interaction with us, and it's likely that consumers will want to be more circumspect about the availability of their data.

Commercial Services

It is likely that commercial services will increase their participation in this area. Already telcos are considering identity management as an adjunct business to be exploited. Banks and utilities are expected to contribute to this growing public service. These companies have a few distinct advantages that position them well in being suppliers of identity provisioning services: they have a lot of information that asserts a user's identity, they are generally trusted, and they have a readily available charging mechanism.

Life Management Platforms

Personal identity provider services are going to become more important. A subset of the population will establish their own identity service with the provider of their choosing, and they will expect government services and organizations to respect and use those services.

A larger proportion of the population will expect government to protect their identity information. The GDPR legislation in Europe indicates the expectation of society.

Identity Data Repositories

Sophistication in the area of identity management will significantly increase. This will be driven by the need to manage relationships in our IdM environment. It's no longer good enough to know a person's identity attributes. We also need to know relationships such as:

- Who are the contacts in supplier organizations, and with whom do our purchasing agents communicate?
- What organization does the company nurse work for?
- Which of our staff have children at the adjacent high school?

In the future, a hierarchical directory will no longer be sufficient. We need to be able to search across relationship "nodes" to form higher-value identity data that provides a more sophisticated, risk-based approach to access management. For instance, if a purchasing agent requests access to the supplier record outside their normal sphere of business, a notification should be issued to ensure that sensitive information about suppliers is not leaked or used for nefarious purposes.

Biometrics

It would be remiss to not consider some of the technology development we are facing in the near future. While in the past biometrics were put in the "too hard" basket, two factors are forcing this technology into the foreground: the falling cost of biometric devices and the increasing need for higher-level authentication. Four technologies are dominating this space.

Facial Recognition

To improve the level of authentication available for corporate applications and the provision of government services, facial recognition is becoming increasingly more accepted. Most adult citizens have a stored facial picture associated with their driver's license. This means that a number of government services can be automated. Authentication mechanisms that use a device's camera and compares the user's image with their stored facial recognition templates will significantly heighten the level of authentication available.

The image can be used for other purposes. For instance, an occupational license that requires an image, such as a security guard accreditation, could access the driver's license repository and use the image to not only authenticate the user but to print on the license, once approved. It is noted that there are policy and regulatory issues to be addressed in deploying such a system, and user consent is required before a driver's license image could be repurposed.

In the corporate arena, inclusion of a facial recognition template as part of the login procedure will become more widespread. It isn't inconceivable that facial recognition should be included in the identity federation task. For example, if a Boeing employee seeks airside access at an airport, a SAML request to the Boeing IdP for facial recognition would be a good idea.

Fingerprint Recognition

Fingerprints are more popular in North America, and the use of fingerprint validation for authentication is on its ascendancy because of the low levels of false positives with this technology. While fingerprints are considered more intrusive because they require the use of a common input device for multiple users, the decreasing cost of fingerprint readers is making the use of personal devices more prevalent for Web and mobile app access control.

Note that there is some confusion about the distribution of "fingerprints." Recent criticism of government agencies for making fingerprint templates accessible to commercial organizations is ill-founded. While fingerprint templates are an identity attribute, they are of no practical use to hackers. They cannot be used for identity theft or even identity spoofing. In fact, it could be argued that, because they have the ability to implement very secure authentication, fingerprint templates should be made more widely available.

Voice Recognition

Virtually all client devices today include a microphone, and voice recognition is well established. Speech-to-text is a mature technology being used for device commands and speech input for word processing. It is a non-intrusive technology that can be used for physical access control and is appropriate for remote access to protected applications. For instance, data entry of a customer order by a salesperson on the road can be used for a non-repudiable transaction with a voice recognition authentication service.

Gesture-based Authentication

The cell phone is so much more these days. And since these devices have generated the "how do I authenticate a mobile device user?" problem, it's only appropriate that they solve it, which they have done. Accelerometer and gyroscope technology is now an integral part of a smartphone. Combining these technologies to recognize gestures provides a high degree of certainty that the user is who they say they are. Gestures made by a user are unique and can positively identify them with a low probability of false positives.

Risk-based Authentication (Identity Analytics)

As the authentication task becomes more difficult, with the need to accommodate access from anywhere at any time by anyone, a more sophisticated approach to authentication is necessary. Whereas the typical basis of authentication has in the past been based on one, two, or three factors: something you know (e.g., password), something you have (e.g. a smart card), or something you are (e.g., fingerprint), a more nuanced approach is coming to the fore.

It is now recognized that the likelihood that a user who accesses a computer system is who they purport to be can be increased by a number of factors, often context based, that are combined to attest to the veracity of the user's identity. For instance, if a person who is accessing a protected resource is using the PC they normally use, at a time they normally connect, from a local IP address, there is a high probability that they are indeed who they purport to be. If the access, even though the username and password is correct, is coming from an unknown device at an odd time of day, or from a remote location, the risk level for access should be raised and potential challenge-response questions should be used.

The ability to use identity analytics for data loss protection purposes will become more prevalent as vendors are increasingly supporting a risk-score approach to access control. Applications and protected resources are assigned a score, and any access to the application or resource must attain the required level before access is granted.

Device Support

A major trend is in the burgeoning array of external devices that users want to connect to systems and applications. Smartphones are becoming smarter, wearables are increasingly being used as interface devices, and IoT sensors are collecting more data. In this environment, password-less but high-authentication access is required. One initiative that has developed solutions in this area is the Fast IDentity Online (FIDO) alliance, a group of companies that have joined together to develop an architecture to provide safe, reliable authentication from external devices. This architecture consists of a software stack that can be incorporated in devices to provide secure communications or in a hardware device to allow users to securely connect to corporate applications from mobile devices. FIDO also supplies code for two-factor authentication, which is a major trend in the authentication industry sector.

Networking

Identity management also has a major effect on network technology. The days of configuring firewalls, switches, and routers to segment subnets is rapidly diminishing in importance. Information technology is leveraging identity management repositories for access control purposes at the application level. Adoption of cloud services is a major driver for this migration, but developments in authorization technology and data loss prevention devices that use access control policy are making OSI level 3 controls less important.

> During a recent natural disaster, clients of a cloud service provider who had indicated sovereign data restrictions on their data, requiring the database to be limited to the local data center, lost access to their information until service was restored. Those that had not indicated such a restriction maintained service from an out-of-jurisdiction data center.

Another major trend that will have profound effect on our technology infrastructure is software-defined networking (SDN). Network device manufacturers are increasingly seeking to offer agile environments that provide dynamic access control based on user attributes. AD groups are often leveraged for this purpose. However, as the technology matures, there will be increased reliance on directories and greater protocol support.

Blockchain

Development of blockchain technology has accelerated, primarily in the financial technology space, over the past few years. It is now well entrenched because of its considerable promise. Blockchain has the ability to irrefutably record the fact that a transaction occurred. There is a widespread misconception that blockchain actually records the details of a transaction. However, this is not the case: it simply attests to the fact that the transaction occurred and when it occurred. This makes it ideally placed to attest to the veracity of a contract. The distributed nature of blockchain means that transactions can be widely distributed; the technology is ideal to record the fact that a transaction occurred, without having to rely on a centralized and potentially remote recording facility.

There is some speculation that blockchain is suited to the identity management task. While it no doubt has applicability to the recording of transactions in the identity management chain of "events," it is not clear how this would assist validating identity data or supporting the access control task. From an identity and access management perspective, blockchain is under a "watching brief."

Conclusion

Identity management will play an increasingly important role in the technology of tomorrow as organizations, both commercial and public sector, seek to improve their online services and make their infrastructure more secure. Access should increasingly be based on identity data, and authentication to protected resources should leverage a user's selected identity provider services.

The public wants to be isolated from the complexity of making this happen. They will expect a website to work first time every time and to accurately determine the level of access they should be granted. For higher-level assurance, the public will accept a second factor but will not expect having to type in the password, or even a PIN. The preference is facial recognition, hand gesture, or a FIDO device.

Rather than a "buyer-beware" approach—whereby users have to be more careful in their use of identity data on sites they access, users will expect, and the government will enforce, a more supply-side approach to security. Collection of identity data must adhere to privacy legislation and must not be abused. Users will expect their data to be treated appropriately and protected sufficiently. Collecting data because you can, in the hope that it might be useful someday, is no longer tenable.

Maybe the best approach is to realize we're all in this together—and together we can make our technology solutions safe, secure, and profitable.

Index

Boldface numbers indicate illustrations and tables.